th
twilight

Arlene Russo

the real twilight

True Stories of
Modern Day Vampires

JOHN BLAKE

Published by John Blake Publishing Ltd,
3 Bramber Court, 2 Bramber Road,
London W14 9PB, England

www.johnblakepublishing.co.uk

First published in hardback as *Vampire Nation* in 2005
This updated paperback edition published 2010

ISBN: 978 1 84454 925 2

British Library Cataloguing-in-Publication Data:
A catalogue record for this book is available from the British Library.

Design by www.envydesign.co.uk

Printed in Great Britain by CPI Bookmarque, Croydon CR0 4TD

3 5 7 9 10 8 6 4 2

Every attempt has been made to contact the relevant copyright holders,
but some were unobtainable. We would be grateful if the
appropriate people could contact us.

DEDICATION

This book is dedicated to Dr Raymond T. McNally and Vincent Hillyer, two Dracula scholars who passed away before this book reached completion. I have no doubt that if they were still alive they would have been a part of this work, with their endless enthusiasm and kindness. I am fortunate that when I first dipped a tentative toe into the world of Dracula studies I met luminaries such as McNally and Hillyer. I could not have asked for more.

Raymond's contribution to the Dracula legend is phenomenal. He was Professor of East European and Russian History at Boston College and the best-selling co-author of *In Search Of Dracula* and *Dracula, Prince of Many Faces*, both historical biographies of Vlad ('The Impaler') Tepes. He was part of a team that discovered the real Castle Dracula in the Carpathian Mountains of Romania in 1969. For years Raymond provided my fanzine *Bite Me* with support and even promoted it in his American homeland. His kindness will be forever remembered. Vincent Hillyer, a respected author, dedicated much time to researching vampires. He was also the first man ever to spend the night in Dracula's real castle in Transylvania. I remember with great fondness the first and only time we met – at a Dracula convention in the US – when he took much pleasure in telling me of his famous stay in the castle. He had obviously told the story many, many times over the years, but he recounted it with such enthusiasm, I felt as if it was the first time he had ever spoken about it. Vincent was the brother-in-law of the Shah of Iran, and it was because of his former ties with Iran that the Iranian ambassador contacted the Romanian ambassador to allow him to spend the night at the famed castle. Vincent was delighted to offer his support to *Bite Me* and his kind correspondence kept me going in the bleak months when the magazine was struggling to get off the ground.

This book is dedicated to their memory.

'YOU THINK YOU HAVE LEFT ME WITHOUT A PLACE TO REST,
BUT I HAVE MORE. MY REVENGE IS JUST BEGUN.
I SPREAD IT OVER THE CENTURIES AND TIME IS ON MY SIDE.'

COUNT DRACULA, FROM *DRACULA* (1897)
BY BRAM STOKER

ACKNOWLEDGEMENTS

As I walked the long, dark and lonely road to complete this book, I am grateful in having many people who helped me along the way. Firstly, I extend grateful thanks to all my readers and contributors of *Bite Me* magazine for supporting me throughout these bleak years as I struggled to run a magazine single-handedly, and simultaneously write this book. A special thank you to Shirlie Leighton, the one true shining light throughout the ten years of *Bite Me*, for always being there and never failing to come to my rescue, and boy did I need rescuing...

Through my studies of the supernatural I have been fortunate in meeting some of the world's greatest Dracula scholars. The knowledge and support that they have kindly given me over the years has been invaluable and so I thank Dr Jeanne Youngson and her team at The Vampire Empire New York, the world's biggest Dracula fan club. I thank Dr Rosemary Ellen Guiley whom I met at a Dracula congress in

Transylvania and personally presented me with her book *Vampires Among Us* which was one of the first mainstream books to explore the modern vampire as a distinct subculture. I wish also to thank my very favourite forensic biologist in the whole world, Dr Mark Benecke. Thanks also to Mick of the London Vampyre Group, for answering every single question I threw at him; sorry I couldn't print every single word you said. Special thanks to very own vampire agony aunt, Katharina Katt, who provided support along every step of the way.

I would like to thank John Blake for believing in me and this book, especially at a time when vampires were not so fashionable. I would also like to thank Clare Tillyer for her support over the years and to John Wordsworth, my editor, for his help and support in this new edition.

I extend grateful thanks to my family and standing by my side in many different ways, even if they would rather I wrote a book about something else! Maybe one day I will... Well, apart from my dear father who never failed in his support of my vampiric writing endeavours ever since he let me stay up late all those years ago when I was a child to watch the Hammer horror double bills.

And how can I forget my twin Anita and also wee Beatrice for their encouragement and lightening the dark days (and moods!) of writing and researching this book.

Finally, a special thank you to Bram Stoker for unleashing your creation Dracula unto the world, without which this book would not have been possible.

Arlene Russo

CONTENTS

INTRODUCTION

Do Vampires Exist and
Mingle Among Us?

Do vampires exist among us? Of course they do.

At the very minute you are reading these words, sanguine vampires are drinking blood, while psychic vampires are draining victims of their energy. In fact, these psychic vampires could be draining you of energy and you may not even know of it...

You will probably be unaware of any of this. Vampires are not likely to run amok, drawing attention to themselves. They have survived for hundreds of centuries lurking in the dark, and I suspect they shall continue to do so.

Discussions of real vampirism tend to focus on medieval accounts of eastern European folklore or obscure cults in America. Vampires, however, do not live in mythical lands surrounded by swirling mists. Vampires are all around us, in shops, supermarkets, the high street, everywhere. They are definitely among us. My journey through the world of vampires certainly shed a few of the myths surrounding this most mythical of creatures. I hope I do not disappoint too much while I shed some of those myths. Did you know that vampires are actually fussy about whose blood or energy they consume? Hell, they might not even like us...

Vampires, I have discovered, are not heartless predators who kill unsuspecting victims before disappearing into the night. In fact, true vampires do not need to kill at all and instead cultivate a relationship with their donor, thus ensuring a regular supply of blood or psychic energy. Vampires that kill are, thankfully, very rare and are more likely to find themselves institutionalised, rather than socially integrated into our communities.

This book is not concerned with debating whether vampires exist. Its starting point is that they do exist. They are growing in numbers and they are here to stay – whether we like it or not. That said, I am often asked if 'undead' vampires, like Bram Stoker's Count Dracula or Anne Rice's Lestat, really exist. I generally reply that if they looked like Brad Pitt, Tom Cruise or Gary Oldman, then I certainly hope so. On a more serious note, however, if undead vampires in either the literary or medieval tradition exist, I have yet to meet one.

In her book *Vampires Among Us*, Rosemary Ellen Guiley declares that vampires do exist 'because we believe in them'. She notes that there are people all over the world who believe they are vampires, and that by acting out those vampire roles they are creating a vampire reality. 'Can we answer the question "Do vampires exist?" ' she asks. 'Yes. Vampires do exist because we believe in them. Vampires exist in subjective reality, the internal landscape of our consciousness. Vampires have the capability of existing in objective reality – the external world – when conditions are right. When Vampire Reality is created.'

Guiley continues:

> The vampire became even more glamorous when Bram Stoker's novel *Dracula* was made into a movie in 1931. A little-known Hungarian actor named Bela Lugosi flashed onto the silver screen as the vampire Dracula. Lugosi cut a sinister but exotic figure, sweeping about the streets of Victorian London in the full evening dress of tails, cape and top hat. He glowered at the lesser mortals he met, seductively drank the blood of young women, and mesmerized everyone, on and off-screen, with his intense gaze and dramatic accent. From then on, fiction and film created a separate stream of the vampire myth. Vampires became less frightening and more sexy and glamorous, peaking in the sensual, beautiful creatures created by Anne Rice in her *Vampire Chronicles* series. The fictional vampire no longer shunned, but emulated. In art, we have lost our fear of the vampire as the personification of fear of death.

So, what is this mortal fascination with the immortal undead? A creature that rises from its grave at night, attacks innocent people while they sleep, drains their blood and destroys them. How did such a murderous reanimated corpse become an icon of our times?

The vampire's appeal is multidimensional. Firstly, the vampire offers the illusion of complete power. Dracula's deep, hypnotic eyes put his victims into a trance that causes them to lose their will. Secondly, immortality is another of the vampire's appealing features. In our society obsessed with looks and beauty, the vampire does not age and is physically frozen at its most youthful. Imagine being able to live forever: one could learn to speak every language, play every musical instrument and travel the world countless times over. In our short, mortal lives most of us barely manage to do half the things we want to. Either we are too young to do these things then all of a sudden we are too old. Immortality solves that. Also, vampires embody the appeal of darkness. At night, the world is quieter and more intense. One can focus on the moment; the immediate sensations of touch and taste, sound and smell become more intense. And finally, of course, part of the vampire's appeal is romantic and sexual. A tall dark figure arrives in your room at night, takes you in his arms and aims straight for your neck. And you are powerless to resist. Fatally attractive, immortal, a mysterious creature of the night, with superhuman powers, Dracula embodies the essence of 'mad, bad and dangerous to know'. He is the perfect stranger. People all over the world fantasise of being bitten lightly on the highly erogenous neck area. The bite, the passionate kiss of the vampire, has the power to change one's life forever. It is transformation through passion.

The appeal of the vampire has increased in recent times, and it is not hard to see why. The vampire embodies feelings of dark romance, mystery and power and offers comfort and hope to people trapped in today's cold and computerised world. And as our world is becoming even more technological, the vampire's appeal can only grow.

In recent polls of the scariest monsters of our time, the vampire languishes near the bottom and, in many cases, does not even feature at all. In *Total Film*'s 'Top 25 Serial Killers' poll in 2002, Hannibal Lector from *The Silence of the Lambs* was voted the most evil murderer. He triumphed over a host of other screen nasties, included Jason Voorhees from *Friday the 13th*, Leatherface from *The Texas Chainsaw Massacre* and John Doe from *Se7en*. In the past, one of these coveted positions would have been claimed by Dracula. But this most favourite of murdering monsters no longer scares us.

The vampire once invoked fear in people who believed that the dead could return to attack the living, and drink their blood. However, in many people this fear of the vampire was to be replaced centuries later by a desire to actually be one. It was in the 20th century that the vampire became fully established as a universal archetype. The vampire permeates our culture. On the internet the vampire has given rise to a whole genre, with thousands of sites dedicated to vampire fiction, folklore and film, among dozens of categories. University students write their dissertations on vampires. The vampire stares out at us every day from the high street in shops selling everything from plastic vampire figures to Dracula T-shirts. We switch on the television to see dozens of new vampire films and endless repeats of old ones.

The vampire has constantly reinvented itself in our culture. From Bram Stoker's Count Dracula in the 19th century who was depicted as an outcast of society, to 21st-century best-selling novels such as those of Anne Rice, the vampire is now fully humanised. Television programmes such as *Buffy the Vampire Slayer* have introduced vampires to a whole new generation and have again revamped the vampire as an urban character with universal appeal.

The vampire differs from others of its kin, such as the *Creature from the Black Lagoon* or *The Mummy*. It is taken seriously. At the end of the first stage performance of *Dracula* in 1924, the actor who played Van Helsing reassured the audience: 'Just a moment, ladies and gentlemen! When you get home tonight and the lights have been turned out and you are afraid to look behind the curtains and dread to see a face appear at the window – why, pull yourself together! And remember that, after all, there are such things!' Indeed there are...

The Real Twilight is concerned with the influence of the vampire on real people and real lives. It is about people who live vampiric lives, people who believe they are vampires, people who want to be vampires, people who know they are vampires, and people who hate vampires.

I use the word 'real' with reference to vampires, to distinguish these 'Human Living Vampires' (often referred to as HLVs) from fictional, or supernatural vampires. Hence, I have avoided deep discussions of mythological, literary, cinematic or role-playing vampires. For the purposes of this book I have refrained from including the category of supernatural or folkloric vampires in discussions of real vampires alive today. So do not expect modern-day accounts of fabulous creatures boasting that they have lived hundreds of years. Such vampires may or may not have existed, but it is not the task of this book to investigate this question further. Firstly, because there are many books that cover accounts of folkloric vampires; and secondly, because this book is concerned with the vampire in contemporary society. (That said, I do discuss folkloric vampires briefly in Chapters 3 and 4.)

I include the category of criminal vampires in this book, but by doing so am not determining their status as real vampires. Again, my reasons for doing so are twofold. In the first place, these homicidal vampires are the vampires that receive the most attention in the media, and indeed whenever the subject of 'real vampires' is raised. The downside of this is that the view we have of real vampires is a biased one, as the media focuses on the vampires that make the headlines – the vampires who murder. *The Real Twilight* aims to give voice to the vampires who do not kill. Secondly it would be pertinent to exclude them in a study of contemporary vampire activity especially when these 'vampires' have a specific connection to the UK, in which the framework of this book is set. Such criminal vampires are generally not welcomed by vampires or the vampire community, and the latter distinguishes and distances itself from these people. Furthermore, I am not a criminologist and the purpose of this book is not to discover why people commit vampire crimes.

Nor is the purpose of this book to analyse causes of vampirism. *The Real Twilight*'s purpose is, rather, an acknowledgment that this phenomenon of vampirism does exist. Naturally, opinions of what constitutes a real vampire are to a certain extent subjective, and my definition of a vampire will always be a personal one. In my categorisation of vampires, I have excluded role-playing enthusiasts, Goths and any others who profess vampire obsession, unless there is a definite crossover to the actual daily lifestyle of the person. A definite life choice must be evident. This was a difficult task, as I have come across many people who were exceptionally eager to be labelled as vampires – I could almost sense the desperation in their words as they tried to persuade me of their claim. These people are known as wannabees or 'vampabees'. And there are a hell of a lot of them out there!

Some declare they hate the sun and always wear factor 30. Some positively hate the sun and only leave the house during the middle of summer with an open umbrella, as 'sunglasses just aren't enough'. Others claim they are more alert as night falls. One told me: 'I've always been fascinated by vampires ever since I saw *The Lost Boys* and since that day I've wished to become one.'

Interestingly, all these wannabees seek to be vampires of fiction and film, not legend. They want to believe in the vampire invented by authors and film makers, not by their ancestors who were terrified of walking corpses.

Then, of course, there are the vampire lovers – those interested in the vampire genre but not necessarily involved in a vampire lifestyle or life. There are many of them. In fact, it is easier for me to remember those who show no interest at all in this genre than those who do. I have discovered, though, that vampire enthusiasts cover all ages and backgrounds, and I am never surprised at those who reveal themselves to be fans. I am actually more surprised when, on rare occasions, people say they hate vampires. It has only happened once – oddly, the person in question was a member of a vampire society.

Regarding the 'vampyre vs vampire' debate: 'vampyre' is the older spelling of the word used in the 18th and 19th centuries. Thus, 'vampyre' is used to refer to people who are genuinely into the scene or lifestyle. The vampire community often prefers to use the spelling 'vampyre' rather than 'vampire', to stress that their lifestyle is a modern form of vampirism, in contrast to a more scholarly take on the genre. Moreover, 'vampire' is frequently used in the context of Hollywood, myth and fiction. In this book, I only use 'vampyre' when referring to the proper names of societies and titles.

No matter how one defines a vampire, it must be accepted that science has never proved that anyone has ever come back from the dead. However, the belief that this undead creature might still exist exerts a powerful grip on our imaginations. Many of us still cling to the belief that such a being might exist.

Let's suppose these undead vampires do exist: imagine how difficult it would be to know what to look for. Over the centuries the vampire has had countless incarnations and permutations. Would this vampire walk in the daylight, or lurk in the shadows? Would he burst into flames at dawn? Can he fly like a bat or shape shift into a wolf? Is he afraid of crucifixes and water?

If you scorn such stereotypical ideas and think you know what a vampire is, ask yourself one thing. Would you know one if you met one?

PREFACE

THE TWILIGHT YEARS

O ver the past few years, vampires have enjoyed a huge surge in popularity. Vampires are everywhere these days. From book-to-TV adaptations *Vampire Diaries* and *True Blood*, to films like *Lesbian Vampire Killers* or the critically-acclaimed *Let the Right One In*, you can't switch the television on, go to the cinema or pass a bookstore without the seductive gaze of a vampire staring out at you, enticing you in.

Topping the bill is the phenomenon of the *Twilight* books and films. It all began in 2003 when author Stephenie Meyer woke from a dream that compelled her to write a story about a very unconventional romance. The four books that make up *The Twilight Saga* – *Twilight*, *New Moon*, *Eclipse* and *Breaking Dawn* – are about an ordinary schoolgirl, Bella Swan, and her vampire boyfriend, Edward Cullen.

It is now very obvious that *The Twilight Saga* is not simply a passing fad of teenage girls. Since publication of the first in the series in 2005, the four books have sold over a staggering 70 million copies worldwide, with 4.1 million copies sold in the UK alone. So far in 2009, a copy of *The Twilight Saga* has been sold in the UK every 2 seconds.

Fans across the globe are now celebrating the series in extraordinary ways: *Twilight*-themed blood drives have been set up independently by charities to increase blood donations; websites have been launched especially for parents to discuss anything and everything about the saga; unofficial *Twilight* proms have been held; and devotees worldwide even commemorate Bella Swan's 'birthday' on 13 September.

The film *Twilight* was released in November 2008 and was a huge hit. It grossed over £10 million in the UK, making it the second highest grossing independent film of 2008. The second film in the series, *New Moon*, released in the UK in November 2009 broke box office records.

But does this proliferation of vampire-themed books, TV shows and films have any special significance in the popularity of the vampire in modern culture? I'm afraid not. There's nothing remarkable about this sudden proliferation of vampires. It happens every generation (even if, previously, they have been a little less media-friendly). After all, in these *X Factor* times, we all know the power of the teen vote.

In terms of *Twilight* and its romantic view of vampires, there is also nothing really new in this. Bram Stoker alluded to the sensual qualities of the vampire (remember that he was bound by conventions of his straight laced Victorian times). Nor must we forget the best-selling author Anne Rice, who explored the seductive element of vampires in her *Chronicles of the Vampire* series.

As far back as I can remember every generation produces a

vampire film that captures the public's imagination, drafting in a whole influx of new aficionados to the genre. In the seventies it was Hammer Horror and Christopher Lee; in the eighties it was *The Lost Boys*; in the nineties it was *Interview with the Vampire* and Bram Stoker's *Dracula* (that was an excellent decade for vampire fans); and in the naughties it was *Twilight*.

Whether your heart belongs to vampires from this decade or from another, it only confirms what I have always known: that for some reason people are obsessed with creatures of the night. It only takes a film or a book to highlight that, opening people's eyes to the vampire phenomenon. Do I like *Twilight*? Well, I'm afraid my heart will always belong to the Hammer horror vampires. Christopher Lee is a hard act to follow. Essentially I believe it is the first screen vampire that captures your imagination and this depends which year you were born. For me I was of the generation of Hammer horror and for those today it is *Twilight*. I have no doubt if I was a teen today – and I wish I was sometimes – then I could well be a *Twilight* groupie.

When I was a child first drawn to vampires, I was captivated but the horror of it, not the sensuality of it, and certainly not the romantic element. At ten years of age I was much too young to even have romantic notions. No matter how much people might like to think my fascination for vampires is a romantic one, it is not; it never has been and I doubt it ever will. It is, I suspect, something darker.

The year 2009 marked the tenth anniversary since I launched *Bite Me* magazine. During that time I was inundated with important works of vampire fiction, none perhaps more so than the official sequel to Bram Stoker's *Dracula* written by his great-grandnephew, Dacre Stoker. Yet, out of all these books, it is undoubtedly *Twilight* that has been the most mainstream, generating phenomenal hype. Perhaps we should be grateful that vampires – and vampire fans – are truly out of the closet.

People ask me if I have seen a sudden increase in vampire fans. Not really. If more people opened their eyes they would see that the vampire craze has always been there. It never went away. Or maybe it just survived quietly without all the teen-driven hype. Vampires have fascinated people for thousands of years, and will do so for many more. What is there not to be fascinated about a creature that never grows old and lives forever? Isn't that what most people really want? The secret of eternal youth? To never die? Let's face it, who doesn't want that?

Perhaps I am fortunate to remember a time when vampires were scary, and for me that will always be what I look for in a cinematic vampire. Essentially a vampire must scare, not be some pretty boy to fall in love with. But that is just my opinion. I guess it all depends on what that person's perception of a vampire is. If people want to see vampires as beautiful, tortured creatures, they will. I just prefer my vampires to be monsters. Perhaps it's time vampires returned to the coffin, not the boudoir.

Vampires have been known since the earliest times and the terror these creatures invoked in early Greek civilization bear no resemblance to *Twilight*'s vampires (or werewolves, for that matter). Would any of our ancestors have been afraid of our modern day Meyer-monsters? Would they have bothered to even record them in their earliest writings?

A recent poll in November 2009 by film buffs confirmed Robert Pattinson's character of Edward Cullen in *Twilight* as number one vampire of all time. The poll, conducted by Pearl and Dean, asked 3000 cinema-goers to name their favourite screen vampire. Christopher Lee was voted second and Max Schreck's *Nosferatu* from the 1922 silent masterpiece came ninth in the poll. Who can say if Edward Cullen will reign as the most significant fictional vampire in history? I'm afraid we shall have to wait another hundred years. Will he stand the test of time like Bram Stoker's famous vampire? His novel *Dracula* has never been out of print since it was first published 100 years ago. Who knows if Stephanie Meyer's work will enjoy a similar feat? Will he be immortalised on screen by almost a century's worth of actors of the calibre of Bela Lugosi, Christopher Lee and Gary Oldman?

But let's put the *Twilight* phenomenon into perspective; I guess somebody has to. Strip away the gothic trappings and it is a teen romance story. No more, no less. This teen Mills and Boon – with fangs – is not exactly ideal reader fodder for whole swathes of the reading population, not least vast numbers of the spectrum of male readers. The same, fortunately, cannot be said for Bram stoker's *Dracula*. Whilst not everyone may have read the original novel, Stoker's iconic novel has transmuted into countless films and books and its appeal is ageless, genderless. *Twilight*, alas, does not. We must remember that.

Rosemary Ellen Guiley, author of several vampire books, the most recent being *The Encyclopedia of Vampires, Werewolves and Other Monsters* (Checkmark Books, 2004) says:

> The new crop of sexy vampires for both adults and teens takes vampires yet further away from their original roots as fearsome, horrific supernatural creatures. I have to admit that I became a fan of *True Blood*, and I am entertained by the *Twilight* and *Vampire Diaries* characters. But none of their

vampires frighten me. All of them have contributed to the de-fanging of the vampire, with heroes who resolutely refuse to consume human blood and who follow human-like moral codes. Even the villains lack the sinister punch of the fictional vampires of earlier times, including the creations of Anne Rice.

This evolution of the nice, sexy vampire has been going on for some time, and there are no signs of it abating. We should start thinking about coming up with a new name for these kinds of vampires, for real vampires they are not. Perhaps we shall soon distinguish clearly among different types of vampires: the real vampires of folklore who rise from the grave; the pop culture vampires spawned by fiction and film; and the growing subcultures of living vampires who base their identities on both of the other two. What a fascinating netherworld, a collision and a combining of traits and beliefs! Who knows where it all will lead?

One can only speculate how many who have latched onto the *Twilight* phenomenon will follow the vampire path. How many will follow their true vampire destiny, long after the hype has died down? We shall see.

For real vampires there is no hype, no fad, it is a destiny that calls them, it is something in their blood...

I do have to warn you that if you are looking for nice stories of sparkling vampires then you will find more than that in these pages that follow. The truth about vampires is far more real than that.

CHAPTER 1

WHAT IS A VAMPIRE?

Katharina Katt is a psychic vampire and also the resident agony aunt for UK magazine *Bite Me*. She has been active in the vampire community for over 15 years and provides advice to vampires all over the world. Below is a transcript of a letter she received some time ago:

Dear Vampire,
    I don't like sunlight and hate garlic. Does this make me a vampire?
    Sincerely, Garlic Hater

Dear Garlic Hater,
    Sorry to disappoint you, but no, this alone does not make you a vampire. There are many normal people that do not like garlic and even others that are allergic to it. As for the sunlight, first you have to ask yourself why you don't like the sunlight. Does it

burn your skin too easily? Are you medically photogenic? If your limbs don't turn to dust immediately when sunlight touches them then I can definitely tell you that you are not an 'undead' vampire. However, many 'living' vampires still live 'normal' lives in the sun. Wearing dark sunglasses will protect your sensitive eyes while using a layer of sun block will protect your skin. This will prevent most pain associated with the sun's rays. Make sure to purchase the strongest strength of sun block available and apply it one to two times a day for normal contact with the sun. Those who have been diagnosed with a medical photogenic condition should consult their doctor for treatment and 'day life' instructions.

No matter how many ceremonies you go to, this will not make you a vampire. Just like no matter how many times a man will put on women's make-up, it will never turn him into a girl. 'Living' vampires, according to the thousands of interviews involving them as to their origins, have given us the theory that 'living' vampires are born the way they are. It normally involves an 'awakening' point in their lives which makes them aware of their condition. The only sources we have as to the 'undead' vampire rising from the grave are the myths recorded in history.

According to myth, there are many things that can turn you into a vampire: being a bad person; working in the sex industry during life; a black cat jumping over your fresh corpse; being bitten by another 'undead' vampire; having sex with another 'undead' vampire; not being buried correctly or respectfully; dying violently and many other variations of occurrences. We cannot know what is true or not, that is why we call it 'myth'.

So, what is a vampire? Do you think a vampire is an immortal soul with large fangs that preys on other mortals for blood? Do you think this creature lives by night and shirks from garlic and crucifixes? Do you think he bursts into flame at the first sight of dawn? Are they amazing creatures with extraordinary powers, who can fly and hypnotise their victims? Or dashing fictional vampires like Count Dracula?

Think again. Authors and film makers over the years have been spurred on by centuries-old accounts of vampires and superstition and have transformed the vampire's image continually. The vampire of literature and cinema becomes whatever its creator desires. Among traditional folklore vampire beliefs, the variety is almost as great. There are stories in which vampires are corpse-like and horrible, others in which the vampire is indistinguishable from other people until it gives itself away somehow.

Indeed, sometimes discussions about authentic vampires become easier if we assert what a vampire is not. So let us separate fact from fiction and dispel some myths along the way.

MYTH: VAMPIRES ARE AFRAID OF THE SUN

False. Many vampires are sensitive to sunlight, but sunglasses and sun protection lotions offer sufficient protection. Although vampires are often more sensitive to the sun, this is because they are more sensitive to all forms of energy, and thus need to shield themselves from excess energy, such as in the form of sunlight. Hence, most vampires find the evening more comfortable. Some vampires claim they suffer from photosensitivity, a condition that can be caused by many things, including prescription drugs. Other rare diseases and skin conditions that have been linked to vampirism include porphyria and lupus. With these illnesses the sun's UV rays cause rashes and blisters on the skin within minutes of exposure and in this way sufferers are often likened to undead vampires, as their skin too reacts severely to sunlight. Despite these similarities, however, people who suffer from these diseases do not turn into dust at dawn like the vampires of folklore.

MYTH: A VAMPIRE CAN 'TURN' ANOTHER PERSON INTO A VAMPIRE

False. Many people falsely believe that vampires can 'make' or 'turn' another into a vampire by means of a bite or the blood of another. Although vampires drink blood, it is primarily for attaining energy for themselves and not to convert or 'turn' another.

MYTH: VAMPIRES ARE AFRAID OF GARLIC.

False. Bram Stoker first established this myth firmly in 1897 with Dracula, by suggesting that garlic warded off vampires. Garlic is reputed to make the blood thinner and this belief, added to the strong-smelling properties of garlic, enhanced the myth surrounding vampires and garlic. Many vampires are fond of garlic and use it in cooking.

MYTH: VAMPIRES MUST DRINK BLOOD TO SURVIVE

False: Vampires drink blood for its energetic properties, but not all vampires seek this type of energy. Some prefer to obtain energy through psychic vampirism, whereby they feed off the energy of others. Those that do drink blood consume very little for their health – about a couple of ounces every few days. In reality, ingesting too much blood will cause a person to vomit.

MYTH: VAMPIRES BITE THEIR VICTIMS

False: Fangs or teeth have little to do with vampirism, and biting is not a method used by most vampires to draw blood – primarily as it is painful for the person being bitten and there are easier ways to draw blood, e.g. with a knife but also because it is illegal. Authors and screenwriters have added fangs to the myth surrounding a vampire – and it is a relatively recent invention, as medieval accounts of folkloric vampires did not mention fangs.

MYTH: VAMPIRES ARE IMMORTAL.

False. Vampires live a normal life span like humans. No person has ever been scientifically proved to have lived for hundreds of years. The oldest person to date lived to be 122.

Dr Jeanne Youngson, president of The Vampire Empire – the world's largest Dracula fan club – has received a great deal of correspondence from vampire fans on the subject of what determines a vampire. Here is one such letter:

> Dear Dr Youngson,
> It is urgent to convey the following information to vampire purists everywhere. Fact one: in all my reading about vampires, which is extensive indeed, I have never seen any reference to the carotids, which are the arteries that run up the side of the neck, the very ones vampires go for first. Anyone

who has been bitten by a vampire, even though temporarily anaesthetised, will later have excruciating pain and may need cortisone drugs to help the inflammation. Have you ever seen this taken into account in any books or films? Fact two: the idea of vampires being unable to tolerate sunlight came from the fertile imagination of Henrik Galeen, who worked with Murnau on *Nosferatu*. Fact three: it was Stoker himself who popularised the idea that Dracula could turn into a bat. Very few vampires of folklore were able to shape-shift and almost none turned into bats!

For most people, the word 'vampire' brings to mind the folkloric or literary vampire. Both varieties were brought to life in film and spurred on by centuries-old accounts of vampires and superstition, aided by authors' and screenwriters' inventions. Folkloric vampires are usually depicted as horribly corpse-like. They shrink from crucifixes, scattered grain and thorn bushes. In the past people believed that the recently deceased could come back to life and feed off them. To prevent this, they placed coins on the corpse's eyelids to stop it from opening them and being able to see. They even nailed the corpse's clothing to the coffin to stop it moving.

Real vampires, according to modern findings, are not a supernatural species that belong to the pages of Gothic novels. Rather the vampire is a real, living human and the only difference between the vampire and its fellow human is that the former possesses a different energy form. The real vampire manipulates and absorbs life force, or 'pranic' energy – the essence of life – from other living things, especially humans. A vampire is thus a person who does not possess sufficient levels of prana for his or her survival; if they do not acquire this prana, they will suffer from headaches, lethargy and depression. A vampire must therefore find a donor for sustenance – this can be achieved by drinking blood or psychic energy from the donor. Few vampires claim to be immortal or invincible. They have a normal life span and suffer illness. They are bound by natural laws. Although many vampires claim enhanced stamina and resistance to disease, they are all essentially human, not superhuman or supernatural.

There are endless categories of vampires – and many new sub-categories are invented regularly, such as medical vampires and astral vampires. Or the aforementioned wannabees, a.k.a. vampabees. According to Dr Jeanne Youngson, president of the world's largest Dracula fan club, wannabees are 'the creeps who want to be vampires, dress like them, pretend to suck blood or actually do it, etc. Most of them are pretty weird.'

For this book I have limited definitions of 'real' vampires to two categories – psychic vampires and sanguine vampires. Psychic vampires are often referred to as 'psi' vampires; 'blood-drinking' vampires are sometimes called 'sanguine' vampires. Psychic vampires obtain the energy they need from absorbing life-force energy, or energy surrounding people. Sanguine vampires feed mostly on blood other than their own and through blood-letting techniques. Some sanguine vampires claim there is a deficiency in their blood that means they need to absorb the missing components in their own blood via a donor. Sanguines use professional sterile equipment to minimise infection and recommend tests for AIDS and other diseases before any blood exchange takes place. Whether in the form of blood or psychic energy, the energy is almost always taken only from willing donors and partners. Donors are often called 'black swans' and are treated with great care and respect by the vampire. The definition of a vampire thus effectively comes down to the way in which it obtains its energy. Sanguine vampires or psychic vampires? Blood or no blood?

So what else defines a real vampire? In addition to a craving for blood, real vampires suffer from photosensitivity and have nocturnal tendencies. Many sufferers of vampirism also claim they can 'feel' (and absorb) the energy in living things around them.

Of course, with so many definitions of a vampire it is not surprising that some people mistakenly believe they are vampires. But in the world of the modern vampire, natural sharp canines and an aversion to sunlight do not a vampire make. People with naturally pointed canines are likely to have them capped or removed by dentists, as they interfere with chewing.

In fact, fangs appear to be an invention from horror films. The 1958 movie *Dracula* (US title: *Horror of Dracula*) starring Christopher Lee was the first English-language film in which a vampire was portrayed with a pair of large pointed canines. As a matter of fact, real sanguine vampires would find fangs more of a hinderance than help. Blood-drinking animals, like vampire bats, bite with their incisors and lap the blood with their tongues, instead of sucking it. Vampire blood-drinkers rarely bite their 'donors' with teeth. Hey use sterile needles, lancets or stainless steel blades instead.

The stereotypical image of the vampire lunging for the neck is therefore a wholly inaccurate one. According to real vampires, biting has very little to do at all with vampirism. Neither does accidentally cutting oneself and licking the blood indicate any vampiric tendencies. Humans used to instinctively lick their own wounds due to saliva's antiseptic properties, and would probably still do so if anti-bacterial ointments had not been invented.

Random attacks by ruthless vampires on innocent mortals are thankfully very rare and belong to the big screen rather than real life. The vampire of superstition and literature is a world away from today's safety-conscious and moral vampires, who are actually fussy about whose blood they consume. A vampire's role has been likened to that of symbiont. In an essay entitled 'Are vampires predators?' on one 'real vampire' website, Inanna Arthen states:

> A parasite which kills its host tends to be inefficient, although most hosts do not thrive under the arrangement. A far more constructive model for real vampires is that of symbiont. The real vampire develops his or her abilities to the point of an equal exchange, a give-and-take of mutual dependency. The real vampire trades healing and revivifying powers for pranic energy, and is able to exploit a wide variety of sources. Ultimately, a real vampire may evolve to the point of being able to live only on food sources that require no living thing to die for the vampire's benefit. This is the farthest away from a 'predator' that you could get.

The Vampire/Donor Alliance is a support group for the entire vampire community, from those who profess a fascination with vampires to those who claim to be real vampires. Mostly American-based, there are two annual Gatherings for all members. When asked 'How do I become a vampire? Are we turned? Do you embrace people, or what?' The Vampire/ Donor Alliance reply:

> 'Embrace' is a term from *Vampire: The Masquerade* (TM) [a vampire game]. There is no turning, no 'dark gift', no crossing over. Either you are a vampire, or you aren't. Since vampirism isn't exactly the sort of thing that people talk about at the dinner table, it being a sort of fruitcake kind of thing, a lot of people don't know that they have this tendency until they encounter another vampire or have a dramatic, earth-shattering experience that makes them suddenly aware of that which they've repressed all their lives. I don't like to use the term 'awakening', myself, because it's twee, but it's a lot more accurate than 'turned'.

How do you become a vampire? Simple answer – you cannot. There is no 'turning', no 'dark gift' nor any 'crossing over'. Either you are a vampire, or you aren't. Vampires are born, not made. Many people believe that they are 'vampire souls trapped in human bodies'. Although vampirism cannot be transferred through one person's blood to another, the vampire can be helped to understand his vampiric path. For vampires it is a life and not a choice.

True vampires have energy needs unlike those of most humans, and the ability to utilise that energy to maintain their health. A vampire is thus an energy feeder with certain psychic abilities that allow for the manipulation of, and the taking and giving of, the life force energy. Such individuals are born with this energy deficiency and gradually, as they mature, show an awareness of psychic ability.

Vampires do not learn their vampirism. Vampirism is present

when a person is born and is dormant until the day that person 'awakens' to it and develops his or her abilities. Some vampires discover their energy needs as teenagers; others do so much later, in their forties. In fact, many vampires are not even aware of the condition of vampirism and do not understand fully why they are attracted to the practice of feeding on blood.

'Awakening' is the term used to describe the realisation that one is a vampire, and the subsequent lifestyle changes that result. Some vampires claim their awakening took place after an accident or after a traumatic event. Some cannot remember their awakening and instead claim to have been born vampire. Others are unaware they are vampires until they encounter another vampire or have a dramatic, earth-shattering experience that makes them suddenly aware of that which they've repressed all their lives. The most common trigger for dormant vampirism is hormones and many vampires become aware of their nature during puberty. In short, a vampire is born a vampire and his or her body actually runs on autopilot until they awaken properly. When first awakened, the person is known as a 'fledgling'. During a period of initiation, the fledgling will have a 'maker', or 'sire'. A sire is a vampire 'parent' who guides the fledgling to his true vampire nature. Vampires generally adopt a vampiric name, usually a pseudonym derived from literature, such as Lord Ruthven or a historical figure like Vlad the Impaler.

Many vampire societies often have to dispel myths to people who are desperate to become vampires. The London Vampyre Group received this query a while ago – it is typical of a great deal of correspondence that they receive:

I wish to be 'turned' into a vampire – how do I go about this?

The London Vampyre Group replies:

It is important for you to realise that, in essence, the vampire is a fantasy figure who exists only in the fictional imagination. Out of all the people we have met who claim they are centuries old, get their nutrition from preying on others, and have achieved immortality, not one has a shred of evidence to uphold their beliefs.

Basically, such people are kidding themselves. For us, the vampire as a strong, independent and romantic character is a fantasy and we strive to realise that as a world within which we can escape. In other words, we can reject what we dislike about the 'real' world by using our imaginations. This can take many forms, i.e. some do role play, some have a pseudo vampire/Gothic lifestyle, some write or create artistically, and some are involved in games which involve drinking of blood. You choose your own alternative. We do not have either recommendations or condemnations, it is up to the individual, but we do insist that the choice of others is respected, and that individuals do not get harmed as a result of our activities. If you genuinely believe they are 'real' in the same sense as, say, Louis and Lestat, in Anne Rice's *Interview with the Vampire* and that people can be 'turned' into vampires, then you do need help, but not the kind we can give. Basically, using your imagination does not have to mean that you become totally gullible.
Sincere best wishes, but keep it real,
Vamp- management.

Richard Freeman is one of Britain's few professional crypto-zoologists. He has travelled the world in search of mythological creatures. Recently, he searched the remote jungles and caves of northern Thailand in search of the Naga, a giant crested serpent. As someone who has dedicated his life to tracking down mythical beasts, he seems the perfect person to ask about what characteristics might be used to define a vampire. He replies:

> There are many people who claim to be vampires. Some sharpen their teeth, some sleep in coffins, some drink blood for ritualistic, sexual, or other purposes. They are NOT vampires.
>
> Like it or not, real vampires look nothing like humans. These would-be vampires would shit themselves if they saw the genuine article. Forget Bela Lugosi, forget the great Chris Lee, and for God's sake forget Buffy. In reality there seems to be two kinds of vampire. The Chupacabra terrorises Latin America from Argentina to Miami. Powerful hind legs, smaller forearms, a head with large glowing eyes and savage fangs, and wing-like flaps under the arms. These beasts are said to drain livestock (and allegedly humans) of blood and remove organs.
>
> My colleague Jon Downs searched for this horror in 1997. In Puerto Rico a vet showed him film of two Chupacabra victims she had examined. The sheep had been drained of blood and their hearts were not beating, yet two hours after the attack they still seemed to be 'alive'. They cried out, attempted to stand, their eyes dilated in light. There is no known biological precedent for this. It is like the vampire curse of its victims

becoming living dead. Perhaps the monster's saliva contains a nerve-stimulating chemical.

The second kind of vampire is more ghost-like. It resembles a cloud of mist, sometimes with glowing eyes at the centre. One theory is that these kinds are etheric revenant of the recently dead that can feed on the life force of the living. It is a kind of parasitic ghost rather than a physical being. The most famous case involving this kind of vampire occurred in the US in the 1970s. After the Vietnam War many of the ethnic Hmong people fled the country and emigrated to America. In 1977 many of these settlers in the US began to mysteriously die. Most were young healthy men. No cause could be found. This epidemic was labelled SUNDS (Sudden Nocturnal Death Syndrome). Some Hmong men, however, complained of a feeling of paralysis at night, and the sensation of some kind of entity in the room with them (visual, tactile, auditory or all three). Could there be a connection?

Researchers discovered that back in the mountains of Vietnam there was a tradition of a nocturnal spirit called a Dab Tsog that sucked the life force from the living. Hamong shamen placated the Dab Tsog with animal sacrifice and rituals. When the Hamong came to the US, most of the tribal elders stayed in Vietnam. Hence, the knowledge of the rites that kept this Vietnamese vampire at bay were lost. In latter years the extended families of the refugees came to the US and the knowledge was once more disseminated. With the ancestral knowledge of protection in place the attacks and deaths dropped off.

Different concepts of what constitutes a vampire have changed at different times and in different parts of the world. While many eastern European countries still consider the vampire to be similar to the undead revenant of folklore, the western world has adopted the Bram Stoker model of Dracula. In folklore, vampires were created in a variety of ways – they might be suicides, blasphemers, children born with hair or teeth, red-haired or left-handed children. Below is a selection of the definitions of a vampire, according to a variety of different people and sources.

'Noun: (in folklore) a corpse supposed to leave its grave at night to drink the blood of the living. DERIVATIVES vampiric/vampirrik/adjective vampirism noun. ORIGIN Hungarian vampir, perhaps from Turkish uber "witch".'

(Oxford English Dictionary)

'All sorts of things happen to people after death. You will sometimes see dark fluid coming from the mouth and nose. It looks like blood, but it's not, it's just the body decomposing. Sometimes, if a body is buried with its hands folded across its chest, it will bloat as it starts to decompose, and the hands move. And if moved, a body emits a sound as gas escapes, like a short moan.'

(Dr Mark Benecke, forensic biologist
and expert in clinical vampirism)

'You meet vampires all the time but not the blood-sucking variety. Some people have a knack of draining you of energy. They feed off other people's energy and can leave you completely exhausted.'

(Craig Hamilton Parker, one of the UK's leading mediums)

'A vampire is an immortal creature who can become so cultured, so learned, that they can exceed any mortal limitation. A wonderful cross between someone who has learned over hundreds of years how to play any musical instrument, to speak any language on Earth, but could kill in an instant.'

(Colin from The Vampyre ConneXion)

'There is a link between premature burial and vampirism in that the famous 18th-century "Treatue concerning the Screaming and Chewing of Corpses in their Graves" by Michael Ranft has been used both as evidence of premature burials (screaming and moaning for help in their coffins and gnawing their fingers and hands in their agony) and as evidence for vampirism.'

(Jan Bondeson, PhD in Experimental
Medicine and author of Buried Alive)

'What is a vampire? That depends on your definition of a "vampire". If you mean a revenant who returns from the grave to feed on the blood of the living, or a supernatural being who lives forever on blood ... There are people who for one reason or another (ranging from psychiatric obsession to a matter of choice) drink human blood: maybe one can call these people "vampires", using a very loose definition.'

(Dr Elizabeth Miller, Professor of English at
Memorial University of Newfoundland, an
internationally renowned expert on Dracula)

'There are two main types of vampires: the "living" vampires, and the "undead" vampires. There are many variations to each and vampire research groups are discovering and defining more with each variation they investigate. A "living" vampire is a person who shows symptoms of vampiric traits. This can involve anything from having a hunger for blood, emotion, or energy, to simply being sensitive to light. An "undead" vampire can be a ghost, demon, or animated corpse or a changeling that can't be killed by normal means. Both "living" vampires and "undead" vampires offer so many variations, it would be hard to give an accurate count of each. However, we can definitely separate them into the "living" and the "dead/undead".'

(Katharina Katt, agony aunt and psychic vampire who has been active in the vampire community for over 12 years)

'A vampire is a supernatural agent or a living person who has the ability to drain the vital life force from a living thing. Supernatural agents are the ghosts or spirits of the restless dead, and infernal entities such as demons or shape-shifting beings. Living people are those who either deliberately, through magic, or unwittingly, through innate supernatural ability, have a negative effect on the energy, health and mental condition of others by drawing off the vital life force for their own empowerment or benefit. The vital life force is the universal essence that promotes health and well-being, and serves life itself. In earlier times, the vital life force was symbolised by blood.'

(Rosemary Ellen Guiley, author of *The Encyclopedia of Vampires, Werewolves and Other Monsters*)

On the internet, the topic of how to define a vampire is the subject of continuing debate. In one sample essay, Inanna Arthen states:

If there are vampires, they might well be expected to guard their secrets well. Hence those who know say nothing, or what they say is disinformation – intended to mislead. Universally, at the lowest common denominator, vampires are very man-like beings, perhaps a cult, perhaps a separate species of hominids or manlike apes, or they might be the result of infection with some sort of DNA-altering retrovirus.

Did you know that there is even a category of 'closet' vampires? These vampires hide their true identities and are fascinated by vampires, visiting vampire websites and reading up on vampires secretly without letting their partners or family know of their interest. Usually closet vampires are closer to wannabees than being real vampires.

And we should not forget 'unintentional' vampires. Such individuals take energy needed by their deficit body without their knowing. Sometimes it takes a while for them to realise they have been unintentionally feeding on their partners and friends.

Perhaps you, who are holding this book, are an unintentional vampire? Or a closet vampire? And if so, perhaps it is time to come out of the closet...

CHAPTER 2

AMERICAN VAMPIRES – THEM AND US

It seems that American vampires are less reticent about coming out of the coffin and some are quite happy even to pose on the cover of a magazine. The first real vampire to front the cover of a UK periodical appeared in the short-lived paranormal magazine Uri Geller's Encounters in February 1998. In an article titled 'The Real Vampires of New York City', Vlad and his partner Sky were photographed over a number of pages. The couple later featured in an interview in the launch issue of *Bite Me* magazine.

Vlad admitted: 'I began feeling vampire urges very young, around the age of four or five. I would hang around and see if the girls in the playground would fall over and so I could go over and kiss their wound to make it feel better. But at the same time I was taking a little of their blood.'

His partner Sky said, 'I feed off Vlad around two or three times a month. Blood is basically my strength and my sanctuary. We only come out at night. We live our life in darkness. We rarely go out in daytime but sometimes we have to. You can't always do a photo shoot at night.'

Vlad admitted to being light-sensitive, stating that most vampires are weaker during the day, hence many vampires seek employment at night. The couple stressed they were not immortal but did believe their souls lived forever. They maintained New York was an ideal city for vampires due to its numerous underground clubs and associations linking vampires, with vampire 'masters' willing to take on new recruits and teach the vampire lifestyle. The couple's final words?

'If you do want to become involved in blood drinking, be careful. Remember that you are mortal.'

Tiffany Tarantula, New York singer of goth band The Nuns, featured on the cover of issue 14 of *Bite Me*. Unlike her British vampiric counterparts, she was proud to revel in her vampire status and had no qualms about being photographed and identified as such. She said:

> I think from earliest childhood I knew that I was meant to be a vampire, just because of my pale skin. The kids at school would call me 'white legs' and 'whitey' and the girls tried to beat me up. In California, everyone is supposed to be tanned, so I was humiliated, until I turned around 14 or 15 and saw the beauty in the pale skin look.
>
> I have always loved vampires and being pale and sort of predatory with men I know that I must be one. I tend to take the souls of my lovers and devour their energy, and then sort of become them. Sometimes this makes them angry. Actually men

seem to get angry with me because I get very
romantic and intense and I think it frightens them.
I become obsessed with them, and then I move on.

As far as vampires in New York, there are a lot of
sort of gothic people that think they have magical
powers, and psychic vampires who take your
energy. But as for real vampires, I think only J. and
myself are real vampires because we takes the souls
of our friends and absorb their youth and energy,
then move on in eternal beauty.

Living in any big city people tend to live too fast
and party and stay up all night. But if you want to
survive, at some point you must sort of hibernate
and take care of yourself. I am actually a health food
nut sort of vampire, and take lots of vitamins and
eat salads and fruit etc. While the others fade away
and burn out, we live on. You must withdraw and
crawl back into your coffin...

The first books to detail modern vampires were all written by
American authors, and published first in America; all of them
focused on American vampires. Norine Dresser's *American
Vampires* (1989) was the first mainstream book to explore the
modern vampire's blood fetishism as a distinct subculture.
This was followed by Rosemary Ellen Guiley's *Vampires
Among Us* (1991) and Carol Page's *Blood Lust* (1991).

That was the nineties – what about now? Don Henrie is a
psychic vampire from San Diego, California. Don is also a
sanguine vampire. He drinks blood and don's daily attire
consists of zombie-style contact lens, two-inch pointed
nails, double fangs and chalked white skin. He was taught
how to manipulate energy and see auras by a practising Reiki

master. In fact, people often complain of feeling faint when he is around and some have collapsed suddenly in his presence. Don, 29, became a cult figure in the US following a reality television stint and was inundated daily with groupies desperate to learn his secrets and buy autographed photos of him nude. He even found people digging through his rubbish in the middle of the night, desperate for souvenirs of their 'master'.

According to the voluntary code of ethics for vampire groups, Don's life as a vampire should be known only to his fellow bloodsuckers. But Don broke with tradition to reveal himself and what it means to be one of 'the Chosen'. Vampires such as Don struggle to live in a world where they must be kept hidden. They are often anxious to come out of the closet and spread their message, and find new recruits. Many are on a mission to spread their vampire gospel to their ever-growing international communes.

Don explains:

> I feel that the time has come for someone to stand up, be proud and let the world know that we vampires are here and have been watching you humans for quite some time. We have also contributed to the world. I am glad to take and hold the torch that will illuminate and make more understanding within the world of the Mortal and Vampire alike. Since I am a person that has a public image, it has enabled me to transgress the average stereotypes and break many negative views. I am looking forward to others of different natures to come forth and present themselves.

Yet vampires like Don know they face difficulties in their task of convincing a sceptical public. For starters, there are numerous Dracula myths to dispel. Don again:

> Many misconceptions come from Hollywood. Vampires are always given a bad press. What people don't realise is that vampirism has religious status and there is a strong code of ethics to what we do. There is a real sense of community and trust and we all reap the benefits of being a united family. Negative portrayals give a negative stereotype. I would like to represent a balance.

Totally nocturnal, Don gave up his job as a microelectronics engineer to spend more time practising vampirism. He never gets up before 4pm. If he ventures out into daylight, he gets burned and becomes physically ill. At night, Don visits grocery stores before retiring to his coffin, an environment he enjoys for its sensory deprivation. He explains:

> I have fibromyalgia, which means I have fewer protective sheaths over my nerve endings. As a result, this makes me hypersensitive. Hence, the coffin helps as it cuts out noise and lets me get a good night's sleep. I have always known that I was different and yet the same as the normal populace. My awakening process was a long and lengthy one, it has taken me many lifetimes to procure. From a very young age within this mortal coil we live in, I have always been interested in the occult and anything that helps fortify my image and spirituality.
>
> The term 'vampire' has been altogether met with

negative connotations within the past. I am here to shed a bit of light upon the subject. I have been met with many different reactions within my life as myself. I have seen everything. I have been around those that seem to not have a good view as to my persona, but I find that it is only so because of a lack of education to the subject. There are also times when I have been afforded much gratitude and comfort, due to the mysticism that follows. Just like anyone else within this bloody ball of earth we live on, I too have to deal with criticism. It will always be there. That doesn't mean that I am going to shrivel up and curl into a little ball for the world not to see.

Given the covert nature of vampires, it is difficult to gauge statistics as to their numbers. But in 2003, at the Edinburgh International Science Festival, David Pescod of The Linnean Society – the oldest scientific society in the world devoted to natural history – presented a lecture titled 'The Rise of The Vampire'. He claimed that 27% of the US population thinks vampires live, move, breathe and suck their victims dry. Following the release of the film *Interview with the Vampire* in 1992, 700 Americans claimed to be real vampires and in Los Angeles alone there were 36 registered human blood drinkers.

The Sanguinarium is a network of individuals, organisations and nightclubs who share a like-minded approach to the vampire aesthetic and scene, and claim: 'The goal of the Sanguinarium is to bring to life the vision of the Vampire Connection as found in Anne Rice's "The Vampire Chronicles", which is a network of "vampire bars" and "safehouses" in which vampires can be open about who they are.' Many American vampires adhere to The Black Veil, a voluntary standard of common sense, etiquette and ideals for the vampire community. (The Black Veil can be viewed in its entirety towards the end of Chapter 14.) Many vampires are also part of an active club scene and these clubs are a very important part of the vampire's life.

The American vampire subculture consists of family-like substructures that were first formed around nightclub events such as Father Sebastian's Endless Night. Places where vampires gather are known as havens and often, to gain access to these establishments, vampires must wear a symbol that identifies them as part of the vampire scene, e.g. a specially made silver ankh. Such items also allow vampires to recognise each other outside the club setting and also make them 'feel more like a vampire'.

Vampire families are called 'clans', and their heads are 'elders'. 'Elders' can be 'makers' or 'sires' (they guide and protect a new person in the scene during their 'awakening', and later). Families of vampires who meet are known as 'covens', and all these families are part of the Sanguinarium, the vampire network. The Family Dentist has an important role in the American vampire community and indeed were the forbears of the vampire community in the first instance. Not only do these dentists make artificial fangs, they also help people to form connections with each other.

German forensic biologist Dr Mark Benecke is currently listed in *Who is Who in the World*, America's leading biographical reference source, for his contributions to forensic science. During the years from 1997 to 2000 he undertook a study on vampire youth subculture in New York City, in the context of criminalistic and medico-legal investigations. He interviewed members of the scene, and attended meetings of the subculture under research, and did not rely on written sources without personal confirmation. He says:

> I am used to performing research in prevailing trends among people under the age of 30 years, and observed in many subcultures that an important aspect of these groups is the lack of traditional family bonds, especially the lack of a functional family (with more than two family members). Youth subcultures buffer the need for living in a trusting and loving group, and the NYC vampire scene is one of the most elaborate examples of how genetic bonds are substituted by interracial, cultural bonds. There are very few cities in the world which have clubs that specialise in the needs of a subculture like the vampire subculture but in NYC you can find these clubs.

Benecke discovered that the Manhattan vampire subculture was subdivided into three main categories: psychic vampires, blood drinkers and S&M lifestylers. While psychic vampires believe they can transfer psychic energy from other people to themselves, the second category of vampires drink small amounts of blood, or suck on the unbitten skin believing that they can taste the blood. Lastly, the vampire subculture crosses over into lifestyles related to S&M (sadomasochistic) behaviour. Benecke continues:

> The Manhattan vampire scene is, in contrast to youth subcultures of earlier times, and compared to the London vampire scene, non-political. Older vampires are hard to interview since they fear exploitation by the media. It is clear, however, that

at earlier times, there was hardly any organisation and support for the vampire lifestyle.

From a psychological standpoint it seems that a number of members of the scene have, on a surface level, depression-like symptoms, or, more unspecifically, personality disorder-like symptoms. It seems understandable that those persons are interested in empowering themselves, i.e., their emotional and social competence by the symbolic ingestion of life energy. It has to be stressed that modern youth subcultures, no matter how extreme they might look to an observer outside the scene, cannot be simply put into standard categories of clinical psychology. The event-like character of many meetings, the family-like organisation and the seriousness of the vampires concerning their chosen behaviour seem to be appropriate and socially acceptable in most cases.

It is important to stress that the clubs are mostly places of entertainment where certain types of music are played, and where a very strict dress code is reinforced. However, there is no, or very, very little blood exchange involved. This has two reasons: a) blood exchange is considered to be something extremely private that a person does not want to perform in public, or semi-public, and b) blood exchange is done by only a few vampires at all. Within some clans blood exchange is done regularly but blood borne diseases is usually considered dangerous. If a person develops a severe neurotic need for blood, the person might not become a member of any clan. On the other hand there are few psychologically balanced vampires who claim to need to drink blood.

The vampire communities are in a way very tolerant, at least against their own needs and related topics. That means that other scenes like the Gothic scene, the S&M scene and others can come into very close contact with the vampire community, and frequently they intermix.

Often there are rigid hierarchical structures. Alexander Warlocke is an 'elder' of one of two courts of The Vampyre Society in Gotham, New York. He explains:

The Vampyre Society in Gotham is varied, as it has undergone many an evolution within the past five years. There are two courts, Society Nocturnus of Gotham (or SNOG) and The Court of Lazarus. Both Courts serve the community in their own way. Both courts are run by a Regent and an Elders Council. Both welcome Sanguines from the Tri-state area and visitors from beyond and both enjoy ambassadors from each other's court. We all share havens, although we meet in differing locations (partly due to stricter laws for the under-21 crowd). But all sanguines meet and share lifestyles, blood (wine), each other (especially at our fetish nights) and support our artistic and professional endeavours (St Eve Fashion shows, Master Steelow's Funhouse and Flesh Theatre etc.). The Current Regents are: Lady Tati (Acting Regent for Lord D'Drennan) for SNOG and Marquessa Magdelena for Court of Lazarus. Both societies have originally evolved from the Court of

Gotham, which was formed in the heady years of 1997, a High Time for Goths and Sanguines in Gotham. We have our various Households and Guilds, each standing for a particular nuance in the Vampyre Lifestyle. We are open to anyone wishing to explore said nuances upon the Dark Path but it is also by invitation only. But All Elders of the Households are easy to approach. Simply come to a haven and seek them out. It is usually good to email ahead as not to alarm the Sheriffs and Guardians of the Courts (don't find them – they will find you) and you will be most welcome.

In 2001, a British television documentary named *American Vampires* was screened. It featured interviews with blood fetishists in the USA – cameras followed a 21-year-old girl named Amanda from a Los Angeles suburb to the Near Dark Pub in Hollywood, a hang-out for LA's vampire enthusiasts where, Amanda revealed, 'Everybody gathers, drinks, has fun, and also drinks blood.' Amanda is a donor and admitted she had been 'donating' blood since she was 15. In the documentary, a young girl follows her out of the bar, then sterilizes Amanda's shoulder with a medical swab before cutting the skin carefully with a hypodermic needle in order to get access to her blood.

Until a few years ago, one of the major events in the vampire calendar took place every Halloween in New Orleans, city of voodoo and vampires: the annual Anne Rice Ball. The German correspondent for *Bite Me* magazine attended the last of these events, in 2001. She recalls:

Firstly, to get myself in the mood, I decided I needed

to soak up the dark side of this beautiful city. I headed for Lafitte's Blacksmith Shop, the oldest pub in town, where I joined the Vampire Theatre Tour of master storyteller Lord Chaz. I revelled in the atmosphere Chaz created, with his spooky stories amidst the historic lanes of the French Quarter. The highlight of the tour for me was when Lord Chaz dug his incredibly long sharp fingernails into his arm and started bleeding. When he proceeded to put his arm to his mouth and began drinking, I fainted! Luckily, Chaz's cute assistants, Randy and Brad, were well trained in fetching ice to cool bumps and I made a speedy recovery.

After all that excitement, I did not feel like going to bed early, so I headed to the Shim Sham Club just around the corner in Toulouse Street for some dancing. There I met Father Todd Sebastian of the Sanguinarium from New York. Todd founded a vampire organisation in New York for people who live the vampire lifestyle or who want to learn more about the vampire subculture. Various households and families offer the possibility 'to follow a dark path of enlightenment which helps him or her explore ways of life long lost to the mundane world'. Todd was in New Orleans for his annual Endless Night Festival of the Sanguinarium. Held in New Orleans because hotel rooms are cheaper and Todd said 'no one wants to come to New York in October when it is cold and rainy'.

The Endless Night in the House of Blues consisted of two events. First the Dark Bazaar, with a schedule of live performers, belly dancers, tarot card readers, storytelling by Lord Chaz, and lectures by Damien Deville, founder of the Vampire Church and much more. The second event of the Endless Night was the Vampyre Ball. A young lady in lion-style make-up won the costume competition and a prize of $250. A fairy by the name of MotherTink won runner-up prize of a free piercing. A couple married live on stage with the 'power of darkness'. Music was provided by live band 'The Cruxshadows'. Maven, a fangmaker from New Orleans, not surprisingly, did a roaring trade. And of course, there were specially prepared cocktails like 'Fallen Angel' and 'Vampire's Kiss'. Finally, it was time for the 'The Annual Gathering of the Coven', the meeting of the Anne Rice's Vampire Lestat Fan Club. I had seen photographs in a book once taken from the Memnoch Ball in 1995 and the Gathering of the Coven in 1996.

More than 8,000 people visited each event. I was amazed at the fantastic costumes. So I expected pretty much the same this time. How wrong I was! The gathering took place in a huge theatre and the few people seemed lost in there. The club even had to sell many member tickets at the door. Author Anne Rice herself didn't have the time to show up either. She was on a book-signing tour. I was trying to get a Rococo costume for this year and in the last minute I chose not to wear it. Thank goodness. I would have been really overdressed. True, there were some people in costumes but not many. I would say there were probably about 1,000 people there. The people were my age (27) and older. Much older than any of the other vampire events I have been to.

Although vampire communities are tolerated in large cities such as San Francisco and New York, it's not the same story elsewhere in America. The first grand-scale event for vampire fans took place in the prairies of Winnipeg in Canada in 2000, and was organised by Pandora of Night Shade Promotions. Pandora is from the prairies of Canada and she began founding a vampire scene there. She was motivated to do this due to a distinct lack of entertainment devoted to the gothic scene and vampire. She explains:

> Here in the prairies of Canada in Religion Central, we have been trying hard to build a vampire scene. So far, there have been only two small alternative events every six weeks and one Gothic bar with only one night a week devoted to the Gothic scene. People hide in fear of being locked in the asylum at the first mention of being vampire. This city holds over 650,000 people and this is why I organised this event as I think this is unacceptable. I began founding the scene here and organised an all-genre event in support of the alternative, Gothic, fetish and especially the vampire community.

How does the UK vampire scene compare with that in the USA? Mick of the London Vampyre Group offers some suggestions:

> Going back through our cultural history, the vampire as known to us is firmly couched in the Gothic literary tradition, which flows from writings from the late 18th century onwards. That cultural context was based in northern Europe and is quite distinct from other literary traditions – even, say, that from

southern Europe. This tradition in turn led to other developments such as the Decadents of the late 19th century. The United States was not a part of this tradition and, being a country made up of successive migrations of different populations, is a mixture of many different traditions, none fully established, but all of them in some kind of conflict or competition. For this, the comedian Eddie Izzard jibes at Americans when he says, 'I come from Europe, where we have history.'

For this reason I find that, when American writers produce Gothic novels, the context is more contrived or emphasised, as if they are required to create a tradition that wasn't really there to such depths – e.g. Anne Rice or Poppy Z. Brite. Similarly, the alternative scene has to strive to make an environment, which is quite artificial. The vampire scene largely has to set up an imaginary network of covens and houses like the Sanguinarians with their Scroll of Elorath. (The Scroll of Elorath, v9.0 – English version, describing the Sanguinarium and Strigoi Vii traditions, philosophies, teachings and ideas.) They clearly need to do this to establish a background and tradition: for us in the UK this is all a bit too unsubtle, plus we have all the trappings of an aristocracy and its structures as an integral part of British society.

Also in the US there is a great prevalence of blood drinking and its importance or significance within the club scene. I think this is another example of their need to be 'obvious' in the outward expression of what you do. In the UK there is more of an emphasis on just doing it all for fun and we do not see ourselves so estranged from society as a whole. Having said all this, my impression is that the US scene is bigger and could possibly be seen as being healthier for that reason.

Dr Jeanne Youngson was the first person to set up a Dracula and vampire fan club in America, in 1975. Although the aim of the club was not to unite real vampires, inevitably some correspondence filtered through that amply highlights the preoccupations of contemporary American vampire fans – and vampires. Youngson observes:

Some of the mail we get is truly unbelievable. I once helped a friend who was handling mail for a rock group, but that was nothing compared to what arrives at club headquarters. For example, 'Edith', a middle-aged woman in Florida, wrote and said she had a big crush on Count Dracula and would we please send her his address? We replied that Dracula was a fictional character and we did not have an address for him. This deterred her not one whit. She began sending explicit love letters to him care of the club, which we returned explaining over and over that Dracula was not real. We were startled to get a call from her two adult children, demanding to know why we wouldn't give their mother Dracula's address!

Here are some letters from Dr Youngson's *Private Files*:

I am 13 years old and very unhappy at home. I would like to become a vampire and move out and never see my folks again. If I leave, they would be sorry.

They cut off my allowance because they caught me smoking pot. Please write to me right away and tell me how to do it.

I am crazy about vampires and want you to send me one as soon as possible so I can give them my blood. Please send one to the address listed above. The house keys are on the porch in the bottom of the mailbox and I am at the end of the hall upstairs. I have a picture of the King – not Dracula but Elvis – on my door so he can't miss me. Please hurry. Thank you for your time.

I am a vampire. I don't like sunlight and I wear black, like black jeans, T-shirts, shoes and coats, all the time. I'm not sure if I am a real vampire because the other day I cut my arm and nearly fainted when I saw blood. Please write me as soon as you get this and tell me if you think I am a vampire, or am I just going through a phase?

Perhaps the lure of the vampire is stronger in America because the vampire is allowed to seep into the American consciousness at a very young age. In today's MTV society, the vampire enters the child's terrain every day via cartoons such as Count Duckula, and continues to feed the child's imagination with Count Chocula Cereal. Unlike Britain, Halloween is a huge billion-dollar industry in America and all-year Halloween shops cater for tiny Count Draculas and mini vampire queens. The vampire continues to be a part of the growing child's world, in a country that is the centre of the world's entertainment industry and through which the vampire has reigned in hundreds of films over the years.

Of course, with America having been online years before the rest of the world, vampire sites have been uniting people there years before the rest of us. With the spread of the internet, perhaps the estimate by science expert David Pescod that 27% of the US population believes vampires exist is a little conservative.

CHAPTER 3

VAMPIRES – THE UK CONNECTION. WAS COUNT DRACULA AN IRISHMAN?

For centuries the UK has boasted strong associations with vampires. This chapter outlines the history of the vampire in British folklore, mythology, literature and cinema. We shall also briefly consider a few more differences between American vampires and their UK counterparts. This chapter also presents an overview of the permeation of the vampire into British culture over the centuries, particularly within the last hundred years. It is intended to provide a framework within which the rest of the book is set.

Firstly, let's meet Kate, a vampire from Surrey:

> I must have come into the world wearing plastic fangs and a long black coat, because I have been interested in vampires since I was born. When I was five I used to love watching Hammer horror vampire films. Count Dracula was my idol. I was not really allowed to watch them, but late at night I would get

out of my bed and sneak into the living room and hide behind the sofa to watch. I remember feeling more active at night and coming alive when it got dark. I was sensitive to the sun, it gave me a headache and made me feel awful. At school I used to get my friends to play vampire games with me but I never told anyone I believed I was one.

As I got older I developed an intense craving for blood. It was some sort of blood lust. I loved eating meat, especially rare steak. I enjoyed biting into the flesh of the meat and I loved chewing it. I had this overwhelming urge to bite... Sometimes when kissing boyfriends I almost forgot myself, nearly sinking my teeth into their necks. I always managed to stop myself in time though my ex-boyfriend Gary let me cut his arm to suck his blood. On a few occasions when my blood lust is intense I have cut myself and sucked my own blood. At other times when I have accidentally cut myself, when I see the blood and smell it something comes over me and I cannot help myself drinking my blood.

A vampire can be a demon-possessed corpse that rises out of its grave at night by supernatural means to suck on the blood of the living, like the famous Highgate Vampire Case. Then again, a vampire can also be a modern-day person who shows symptoms of being a vampire – e.g. having real fangs, nail-like talons, sensitivity to sunlight, a need for blood etc. I believe real vampires exist, there is too much evidence and fact to deny their existence. To me, a vampire is a creature that is misunderstood, a creature who has a bad reputation from myth and legend ... But we cannot recognise them because they are too similar to us humans and have adapted – for example, they can go into the sun.

I think it is the erotic angle of vampires that appeals to me. In vampire movies the leading vampire always gets the girls by putting them under his spell, then he seduces them. I see Dracula as being a great seducer... I admire Louis in *Interview with the Vampire*, who kept his human heart. He is romantic and sensitive. He regrets being a vampire but as time goes by he learns a lot from the experience. He learns to appreciate life the way he never did when he was human, to appreciate the most simple things like colour, sunlight and nature, because one day he would lose all this. Vampires like Louis are creatures with feelings, not simply blood-sucking monsters.

The story makes you feel sorry for this type of vampire. We become seduced by the romanticism and it is almost a deliberate effort to keep it as fantasy, not breaking the spell. We are intelligent enough to know that the reality of being a vampire can never be as beautiful as the myth, with the curse of being undead and the curse of loneliness. I have often dreamed of having immortal life and to be able to feel the power that surges through the body. I wish and dream I had my own coffin, a supply of willing blood donors and having a sexy vampire boyfriend. I love to dress in black. It feels powerful, like I'm a vampire and I want the world to know it ...

It is unfortunate that I do not know of anyone like myself. I wish I did, as it gets lonely not having someone to turn to for support and friendship. Ideally I would like to have a night job. I have been to a couple of Vampyre Society meetings, but the people who attend them do not practise vampirism. They only dress up as vampires. I find that blood fetishism is more widely accepted in America than anywhere else ...

Unlike Don Henrie, the American vampire discussed in the previous chapter who is motivated by a mission to spread his vampire gospel, Kate prefers to keep her vampiric feelings secret. While she does like wearing black, she avoids drawing attention to her vampire status and shuns anything as obvious as Don's contact lenses and sharpened canines. Many vampires like Kate have not taken their vampiric interests further and have not attempted to find others of their kind; others are already practising vampires.

The nearest British equivalent to the vampire 'families' of the American Sanguinarium are vampire societies – though blood drinking is not a part of their set-up. British vampire societies are primarily social gatherings that attract vampire lifestylers and wannabees as opposed to real vampires. These societies lack the rigid structures of the Sanguinarium, with its distinct group hierarchy. Nor are vampire belief systems essential – no existing British vampire society indoctrinates their members with codes like The Black Veil. Real vampires thrive in the underground vampire club scene in America; vampire societies here rarely harbour real vampires.

Certainly, British vampires are a lot more reticent than their American cousins. The media has a difficult time persuading them to air their views on camera, and often has to resort to interviewing American vampires. However, the purpose of this book is not to delve into categories of contemporary American and British vampires and argue why they differ. Rather, it is to demonstrate that the British vampire has his/her own identity and is not merely an extension of the American version.

The vampire, we shall discover, is part of British folklore, history, geography, literature, cinema and popular culture. Even our own royalty is not immune to the lure of vampires. Furthermore, the vampire has been a part of British culture for centuries, as the following chapters in this book will demonstrate. From the story of the Highgate Vampire to folklore accounts of vampires, the vampire has escaped from the pages of a book or tales of legends to seek solace in British terrain, and is even celebrated in the form of Dracula tourist spots.

The vampire has a strong role in the literary landscape of Britain thanks to the most influential book ever on vampires, Bram Stoker's *Dracula*. Towns such as Whitby and Cruden Bay, both featured in the novel, boast a thriving Dracula tourist industry. Bram Stoker's novel is also strongly associated with London and Highgate Cemetery is reputed to be the setting chosen by him as the burial place of Lucy Western in the novel. Indeed, the crypts of Highgate are believed to have inspired the scene in which Professor Van Helsing breaks into Lucy's tomb and decapitates her – witness the following extract from *Dracula*: 'A lordly death-house in a lonely churchyard, away from teeming London; where the air is fresh; and the sun rises over Hampstead Hill, and where wildflowers grow of their own accord.'

Unlike America, Britain provides a fertile ground for the vampire traveller, and specific locations have been imbued with vampiric significance. America can only lay claim to haunts of modern-day vampires in pubs and clubs frequented by vampires and lifestylers, or perhaps content herself with fictional locations like Anne Rice's New Orleans, the setting for *The Vampire Chronicles*. By contrast, Britain's rich folklore and history provides a rich backdrop for the vampire traveller that exists outside the pages of a fictional account. Indeed, the UK boasts a rich selection of place names that have become part of the folklore and history of vampires, places where real vampires are believed to have existed.

In medieval times, many countries throughout the world suffered epidemics of vampire attack and most of Europe was under the influence of vampire plagues. In the 12th century, William of Newburgh's 'Chronicles' recorded several stories of vampire activity in England. In fact, from medieval times to more recent times the vampire has often sought solace in the UK landscape. The vampire legend has long been a part of European folklore and although vampiric activity was most prevalent in eastern Europe, the UK was not exempt from tales of blood-suckers terrorising citizens, as we shall see. This chapter and the following include selected accounts of vampires from past times. They are by no means a comprehensive account of vampire activity in the UK, though one could comfortably fill the pages of this book with such accounts.

We shall start with the most famous vampire of all – Dracula. This fictional figure is reputed to have hailed not from Transylvania at all, but far closer to home. In an article in the Summer 2000 issue of the journal *History Ireland*, Bob Curran asks 'Was Dracula an Irishman?' In the north Derry area of Ireland, in a district known as Glenullin, is an area known as the 'Giant's Grave'. On this grave is a thorn bush under which lies a large heavy stone. During the 5th and 6th centuries this area was divided into kingdoms, each with its local ruler. One of these rulers was Abhartach, supposedly an evil and powerful wizard. His evil was such that those he ruled over wished to kill him, and persuaded another chieftain to attempt his murder. Abhartach was killed and buried standing up in an isolated grave. However, the day after the murder, Abhartach returned and demanded a bowl of blood drawn from the veins of his subjects. The terrified locals asked the chieftain to kill Abhartach again, which he did, but next day Abhartach returned once more and again demanded blood.

The baffled chieftain consulted an early Christian saint, who told him that Abhartach was a Dearg-Dul – a blood drinker or vampire. The saint told the chieftain that he must slay the vampire with a sword made from yew, bury it upside down in the earth and sprinkle thorns around the grave before finally placing a heavy stone on top. This would prevent the vampire from escaping but, according to legend, should the stone ever be removed the vampire would walk the earth again. Today the stone remains and a tree has grown from the scattered thorns. But the land on which the grave stands has developed a sinister reputation over the years. In 1997, workmen who were attempting to clear the land discovered that their new chainsaws inexplicably stopped working when they tried to cut down the tree. When one labourer tried to lift the stone, a steel chain suddenly snapped and cut his hand, causing blood to soak into the ground.

Irish folklore is not just confined to the story of Abhartach, as described above. Indeed, Irish folklore is very rich in vampiric entities. The Dearg-Dul is an Irish vampire ghost whose name means 'Red Blood Sucker'. This vampire appears as a seductive woman who rises from the grave at night to entice victims in a deadly embrace. Another Irish vampire is the Leannan-Sidhe, whose name means 'Fairy Mistress'. She is a beautiful faery-woman who takes a mortal man as a lover, marries him and lures him into the underworld of the dead to dwell with her. The Fairy Mistress sometimes shape-shifts into the form of a white fawn and accompanies her lover in this guise.

There are many legends of vampires in the UK, some of which date back centuries. Highland vampires are one of Scotland's oldest vampire myths. The vampire known as Baobhan Sith supposedly haunts lonely spots in Ross-shire, where she appears as a beautiful young woman dressed in green with long golden hair; she preys on hunters and young men trapped in the wilderness after sunset. The Baobhan Sith uses her extreme beauty to lure men into her embrace before attacking them and draining their bodies of blood.

These dreaded vampires of the Highland glens are depicted in the newest addition to gory tourist attraction the Edinburgh Dungeon, with the seductive banshees of legend now celebrated in a £100,000 exhibit entitled 'Vampires: Fact or Fiction'. Edinburgh Dungeon boss Andrew McDonald explains:

> We've done a fair bit of research on the Baobhan Sith, and no one seems certain when or where the name first appeared. The most common tale refers to four men sheltering in a small cottage after a day's hunting in the glens. One of them sings as they warm themselves around their fire, encouraging the others to dance. When one man bemoans the absence of women to dance with, four women appear at the door and join in, but they suddenly turn on the three dancers and start ripping their flesh. Only the singer escapes, taking refuge between the horses, which

keeps his pursuer at bay. As dawn breaks, the Baobhan Sith disappear, but when the singer returns to the cottage he finds his companions dead... their bodies completely drained of blood. The night the Baobhan Sith feasted on the huntsmen is re-created as part of the new Dungeon show.

The vampire has a significant role in the cultural landscape of Britain. Fictional vampires began making their mark in early 19th-century literature. 'The Vampyre', by Dr John Polidori, was published in April 1819 in New Monthly Magazine, and was the first piece of vampire fiction in English. In the 1840s, Varney the Vampire, a 'penny dreadful', was published, eventually running to 109 weekly instalments. This was followed at the end of the century by the single most influential book on vampires: Bram Stoker's Dracula. Since its publication in 1897, the novel has never been out of print. Moreover, since 1992 at least two new Dracula or vampire novels have appeared every month; more than 60% of vampire novels have appeared in the last 30 years.

The film *Dracula*, starring Bela Lugosi, was released in 1931 and spawned a Dracula film industry across the world, with hundreds of movies released about vampires and their kin. Over 700 vampire films have been made to date, more than 100 of which featured the character of Dracula.

The vampire acquired a new home when the centre of the vampire film industry switched from Hollywood to England in the sixties. Hammer Films, famed for their Gothic horror films, launched the careers of a number of stars, including Peter Cushing and Christopher Lee. (Many of these films were shot at Bray Studios near Windsor.) Hammer delivered a vivid, Technicolor package that audiences had not seen before. Their films enjoyed great popularity with audiences, especially because they acknowledged the sexual themes that underlie much Gothic horror but which had been repressed in earlier horror movies.

Christopher Lee, Hammer's leading Dracula actor, became an icon, the quintessential vampire of our times. Lee starred in seven Dracula films for Hammer. He first appeared in the lead role of Dracula in 1958 and became an instant sex symbol as the demonic count. Despite the fact that Lee only speaks 13 lines and appears onscreen for a total of seven minutes in that first film, his portrayal of the quintessential vampire has endured for decades.

By the seventies, Hammer was churning out a new Dracula film each year, in addition to other vampire films: indeed, 1970 alone saw the release of The *Vampire Lovers*, *Lust For a Vampire* and *Countess Dracula*. The last two Lee-Dracula Hammer collaborations brought the Dracula character to London, with *Dracula AD 1972* (1972) and *The Satanic Rites of Dracula* (1973). In the latter, originally titled *Dracula is Dead and Well and Living in London*, Dracula is a Howard Hughes-type tycoon planning to release a deadly new plague virus to modern London. So not only is production of this iconic vampire filmed in an English studio, but the film's narrative brings the vampire character into seventies Britain, well away from its legendary home of Transylvania.

In the late seventies, a new vampire phenomenon emerged. After the success of Anne Rice's 1976 novel *Interview with the Vampire*, many of her readers developed a yearning to be a part of this seductive nocturnal world and sought to re-create the lifestyle of the vampire. Rice's books inspired many vampire events, such as the aforementioned annual Anne Rice Ball in New Orleans. Gothic shops began to cater for these dress-up vampires, with elaborate costumes inspired by Rice's characters. The novels effectively spawned their own vampire subculture, with fan clubs, meetings and eventually websites devoted to the cause. In America, vampire balls and events formed and the vampire lifestyler was born – people who adopted only the outward aesthetics of a vampire. Soon this would cross the Atlantic and vampire lifestyle societies would flourish here too.

Following the popularity of Rice's books, vampire fiction soon became a literary genre in its own right, with special sections of bookshelves dedicated to vampires in the 'occult' and 'horror' categories. Many UK authors too began building a cult following as vampire authors. One of them is Freda Warrington, author of the best-selling Blackbird fantasy novels. She has also written dark fantasies, including a sequel to *Dracula*. Her book *Dracula, The Undead* follows on from Bram Stoker's famous novel and sees the vampire reanimate himself and pursue the Harker family to London, where he continues to torment them. *Nosferatu* (1922) had provided the first cinematic portrayal of Dracula, but it was only after the Hammer horror films of the sixties and seventies and Anne Rice's *The Vampire Chronicles* that fans began to form regular social gatherings and to dress themselves like vampires.

Vampire lifestyle societies first formed in the UK in the eighties and reached their peak in the early nineties. The Dracula Society was formed in October 1973 to cater for 'lovers of the Vampire and his kind – werewolves, mummies, mad scientists, and all the other monsters spawned by the Gothic genre'. A key function of the society was to enable members to meet and travel to regions such as Transylvania, which had scarcely been touched by package tours at the time. The society's emphasis is on London-based meetings, which include guest speakers, talks, quizzes, film and video screenings, auctions, and trips to places with Gothic or supernatural associations. The society stresses it is not concerned with psychic research or occult ceremony of any kind. The other main UK academic society is the Bram Stoker Society, which was founded at Trinity College Dublin in 1980 to promote the study and appreciation of Stoker's works and his influence in the areas of cinema, music and theatre.

In the nineties, a new type of society shifted the focus from academic Dracula groups to vampire lifestyle organisations. Lifestyle societies like the Vampyre Society illustrated perfectly how the vampire had transgressed from folklore, literature and cinema into the psyche and lifestyle of people throughout the UK. It was no longer enough to read about vampires or watch them on screen – now people wanted to look like them and, to a certain degree, act out the lifestyle.

The Vampyre Society was formed in 1987 in West Yorkshire. At its peak it boasted over 500 members and had many branches in cities throughout the UK. Spurred on by the release of films like *Interview with the Vampire*, vampire societies and lifestylers grew in numbers as a whole new generation received its introduction to the genre.

During the eighties in Britain the Gothic music scene developed, a particular style of rock music that often evokes bleak imagery. The first generation of Goth emerged in the UK in the late seventies as an offshoot of the punk movement, inspired by bands such as The Damned and Siouxsie and the Banshees. Goths wear dark clothing (primarily black and purple) and, appropriately, embrace the darker aspects of life that traditional society either ignores or rejects. Many Goths share a natural resonance with the figure of the vampire through their funereal style of dress and – at the risk of generalising – a more morbid outlook on life.

The early 1990s saw the first appearance of vampire websites. One of the first and most popular was Pathway to Darkness, and although it was an American site its resource pages were used as a reference source for many UK vampires. Following the popularity of role-playing games in the 1980s, White Wolf launched the game *Vampire: The Masquerade*. Its game book contained a detailed presentation of vampire clans, legends and game rules. Game players pretended to be vampires and dressed in vampire costume. The same decade also saw the debut of *Buffy The Vampire Slayer* on mainstream television and introduced a whole new generation to vampires, having a particularly strong impact with teenagers. The cult TV show about a California cheerleader's crusade against the undead spawned websites, novels, comics and conventions. The show even spawned its own language, known as 'Buffyspeak', as the show's writers played with language by fabricating new words and morphing existing ones. New words included 'Buffyatrics' (older fans of the show) and 'Franken-Buffy' (monster in the guise of Buffy), while the show also inspired a host of catchwords, such as 'lunchable' and 'über-nerd'.

But the greatest outbreak of vampire mania was yet to come. In 1992, Francis Ford Coppola's production, *Bram Stoker's Dracula*, hit cinema screens and introduced Gary Oldman as the Count in debonair attire. Two years later the novel *Interview with the Vampire* received a lavish screen adaptation with Brad Pitt and Tom Cruise, and the stage was truly set for vampires to come out of the closet. Never before had these legendary creatures looked so glamorous and enticing. Vampire fever had arrived. The press was awash with stories of vampire fans bedecked in sumptuous velvets and laces. The nineties were heady times for vampires – but they were not to last.

In 2001, vampires hit the headlines like never before. A series of real 'vampire murders' within the space of 18 months damaged the image of the vampire's real fans. Criminals had perverted the image of the vampire by performing serious crimes that involved a vampiric side. Vampire fans tried in vain to salvage their damaged reputation at the hands of an imbalanced minority, to convince the public that reading Anne Rice novels did not make them a bloodthirsty menace. In these first years of the 21st century, vampires have retreated even further into the closet.

Today, vampires have found solace in a huge community that crosses continents and geographical boundaries, and through which they receive training and obtain resources: the worldwide web. And vampires are growing in numbers. In an article in the *Sunday Herald* from October 2003, Dr Glenice Byron, who teaches at the UK's only postgraduate course in Gothic Imagination at Stirling University, stated:

> The UK is heading for a resurgence in vampire culture. Far from retreating into the darkness, vampirism in its most innocent form is set to become as big now as it was in its primitive beginnings. It's reviving again now. We are moving towards another high point in vampirism. Why it has come back now, we've yet to find out. But what is certain, is that since the late 1970s vampirism has never really gone away.

CHAPTER 4

FROM ROBIN HOOD TO ROYALTY – OUR BLOODY VAMPIRE HERITAGE

Did you know that Robin Hood might have been a vampire? Or that Prince Charles is a direct descendant of Vlad the Impaler? Or that Queen Victoria and Count Dracula share many traits?

Some of the most famous vampires in history, and most documented accounts of them, belong here in the UK. This chapter will reveal that royalty is not immune from the curse of the vampire. Through their royal blood has flown vampire blood. Indeed, Britain boasts a rich vampire heritage. No longer does the stalking vampire automatically conjure up an image of the Carpathian Mountains, old streets of New Orleans or distant lands beyond the forest. The vampire lives and breathes in our own land, and has done so for centuries.

In recent years, one historian who was examining royal family trees uncovered evidence which revealed that Prince Charles is a direct descendant of the 15th-century medieval Transylvanian ruler Vlad the Impaler – via Queen Mary, consort of George V. Vlad is believed to have murdered hundreds of thousands of Turkish warriors in battle and gained notoriety by impaling his victims and eating bread dipped in their blood. Vlad was also known as Vlad Dracula (Dracula actually means 'son of the devil' in Romanian). Centuries later, Bram Stoker drew on the myth of Vlad to create Count Dracula. Prince Charles is apparently aware of the potential relationship between his family and Vlad. There was amusement in the tabloid press when this family history was revealed, with photos of Prince Charles mocked up with cloak and fangs. At the time, the Scottish Vampyre Society issued a statement to the effect that Prince Charles would have been welcome as a new member.

One disease commonly identified with vampires is porphyria, and this rare blood disorder is believed to have run in the British royal family. Indeed, according to medical research, the vampires of folklore could indeed have once existed, but rather than taking the form of monsters or reanimated corpses, they would have been victims of porphyria – exceptionally sensitive to sunlight and forced to avoid daylight, as any exposure caused their skin to be disfigured by sores, scars and excessive hairiness. Comparisons with vampirism are inevitable, as in some cases the skin of the lips and gums stretched and tightened, making the teeth look like fangs. In extreme cases of porphyria, victims suffered facial deformities, photosensitivity, madness, and finally death. In recent years, George III's madness has been attributed to porphyria. Likewise, the physical symptoms of porphyria are similar to those experienced by his son, the Duke of Cumberland, who suffered from a 'red-mottled face'.

Queen Victoria and Count Dracula are believed to share many traits, including morbid feelings of melancholia and a marked attraction towards other people's throats. Queen Victoria also enjoyed visiting tombs and grave sites, especially the mausoleum at Frogmore, where Prince Albert was buried. In *Victoria's Dark Secrets: A Curious Chapbook & Hysterical History*, author Ed Sams observes:

> As for necromancy, Queen Victoria's divination with the dead accompanied by John Brown and Robert Lees has come to be accepted as common knowledge. Though not accepted historically, persistent rumours claim that contact with Prince Albert was made in which the dead consort would return upon her command. Also noteworthy is Queen Victoria's attraction to throats. On February 11, 1840, the day after her wedding to Prince Albert, Victoria penned in her diary: When day dawned (for we did not sleep much) and I beheld that beautiful angelic face by my side, it was more than I can express! He does look so beautiful in his shirt only, with his beautiful throat seen. We got up at 1/4. When I had laced I went to dearest Albert's room, and we breakfasted together. He had a black velvet jacket on, without any neckcloth on, and looked more beautiful than it is possible for me to say.

Moreover, Prince Albert demonstrated some parallels with the fictional Count, as Sams notes:

> Dracula despised mirrors, for being soulless, he had lost his reflection. Near death, Prince Albert became frightened of mirrors and the visions he saw in them. Lady Elizabeth Longford writes, 'He could see the Blue

Room reflected in a mirror and thought that he was back in the nightmarish gloom of Holyrood Palace [Scotland]. She had his pillows lowered so that the mirror and its ghoulish reflections were out of sight.'

In one section in Bram Stoker's *Dracula*, Dr Van Helsing presents a list of definitive traits of the vampire: 'necromancy ... he can direct the elements; the storm, the fog, the thunder ... he can at times vanish and come unknown'. The first of these, necromancy, finds something of an echo in Queen Victoria's divination with the dead. As for directing the elements, there is a legend about the queen that also provides a tantalising connection: supposedly, no matter how inclement the weather conditions might be, the queen had only to order a perfect day, and that glorious sunshine arrived right on schedule. On the morning of Victoria and Albert's wedding, biographer Cecil Woodham-Smith relates, 'Dreadful day, torrents of rain, and violent gusts of wind.' Later the day cleared and brilliant sunshine broke through – indeed, sunshine was so regularly attendant on the Queen's activities that it was known as 'Queen's Weather'. As for vanishing, Queen Victoria lived out a life of remote seclusion in order to mourn the death of Prince Albert and commune with his spirit. For more than ten years, her subjects were denied any public appearance of their queen, and even after opening Parliament in 1871, Victoria disappeared from public record due to a bee sting. Well, the bee sting was the official explanation for her absence, but Stanley Weintraub, Queen Victoria and Prince Albert's biographer noted: 'Given the severity of her complications – for one reason or another, she was incapacitated for nearly three months – the record is puzzlingly thin, with much evidence of cover-up. Mysterious in her comings and goings, and inscrutable in her disappearances, the Queen caused her prime minister, Gladstone, to remark, "The Queen is invisible."'

Just as Transylvania witnessed a flurry of cases of vampirism in medieval times, a similar thing was happening in the UK. Northumberland proves to be a hotspot with several accounts recorded by the English chronicler William of Newburgh (1136–1198). In his *Historia rerum Anglicarum* (History of English Affairs), three chapters focus on vampires. According to legend, a vampire – or rather the demon of a former wicked lord – lived at Alnwick Castle. At night this demon would emerge from beneath the castle and attack the local villagers who would collapse and die after inhaling the demon's spirit. This vampire terrorized the town of Alnwick, spreading its plague and eventually spurred the villagers to exhume the corpse. But on opening the coffin, they were horrified to discover that the body was engorged with blood. The terrified villagers burned his mortal remains and so put an end to the plague and deaths.

Newburgh recorded another similar case in Berwick-upon-Tweed, of a wicked man who returned to haunt the living after his death. Again, the villagers, fearful of another plague outbreak, dug up the man's body and destroyed his remains.

The final vampire account recorded by Newburgh took place in Melrose in the Scottish Borders. This vampire was reputed to have been a priest at Melrose Abbey who had had a fondness for liquor. Shortly after his death, locals were stunned to see him wandering the cloisters. The proceeded to hunt him down and, similarly, when his coffin was opened they found a fresh corpse, which they hastily burned.

There are even vampire elements in the story of one of Britain's best-loved folk heroes. Deep in the heart of an ancient woodland in West Yorkshire, hidden beneath a formidable barrier of fierce thorns and dense undergrowth, there is a hidden grave. Many people believe that this is the final resting place of the mortal remains of Robin Hood, slain by the prioress of Kirklees Nunnery 600 years ago, and cast into an unhallowed grave. The circumstances of Robin Hood's death are fairly well known. Realising he is dying, Robin decides to be bled by his kinswoman, the prioress of Kirklees, a woman 'skilled in physic'. However, on the way he meets an old hag who curses Robin and on arrival at the nunnery, the prioress proceeds to bleed Robin accompanied by her lover, the convent priest Red Roger of Doncaster. Why did the prioress kill Robin?

Venesection, or 'bleeding', was common medical practice in the Middle Ages. Many people must have died as a result, but it was an ignominious end for the swashbuckling Robin, whether by accident or design. If he was murdered, for whatever reason, it was a particularly gruesome act. It has even been suggested that the symbolic spilling of his blood implies that Robin's death could have been linked with pagan sacrifice, or vampirism.

The past few years have seen reports of paranormal phenomena at Robin Hood's Grave. One of the earliest stories was from an elderly lady. She and a friend often heard Robin calling for Marian over Kirklees, which was just down the hill, and on one occasion they found a silver arrow near the grave. In 1984, a woman called Barbara Green, who visited the grave through her association with the Yorkshire Robin Hood Society, had a strange experience there:

> I knew something strange was happening, then I saw them, at first as flittering almost amorphous forms, merging with the mist which had suddenly coiled

even thicker around the trees. There were two distinct forms that I had no trouble recognising as the Prioress of Kirklees and her lover, Red Roger of Doncaster. Like a bat she hung there for what seemed like an eternity, her black nun's robes flapping eerily while her eyes flashed red and venomous and her teeth bared, sharp and white between snarling blood red lips. Her lover, Red Roger, remained behind her, his crimson-clad figure contrasting drastically with her black one, his murderous red hair stood out from his head like rampant flames.

However, the most enigmatic and controversial paranormal phenomenon was reported by a famous vampire hunter, who masterminded an unofficial mini exorcism at the gravesite in 1990.

In 1990 he and two assistants visited the grave. Apparently one of the helpers became so frightened as they entered the woods around the grave, that he fled into the night, passing the blood drained, dismembered corpse of a goat on the way. Nothing else of note happened on the night, and as dawn rose, the group blessed the grave with holy water and placed garlic in the ground all around it.

The vampirism associated with the legend of Robin Hood stems from the fact that he was bled to death and also the fact that the woman who murdered him might have been a vampire. Also significant is the fact that as a murder victim Robin Hood was buried in unconsecrated ground. As vampire lore dictates, this fact alone could have made him a vampire.

The mystery of Robin Hood's Grave remains unsolved at the present time, though it is far from forgotten. Yorkshire's own 'vampire' is to get a starring role in the latest horror show at macabre tourist attraction The York Dungeon. The new exhibition, 'Vampires: Fact or Fiction', examines the legend of the infamous Kirklees Vampire ... a dark figure of a woman allegedly sighted many times at the Kirklees Priory.

In the early 19th century, the Vampire of Croglin Grange appeared to a family that had rented a remote country house in Cumberland. A female member of the family was attacked by a hideous vampire monster as she lay in her bed one night. The woman witnessed a figure with red eyes scratching at her window; a creature with a 'hideous brown shrivelled face, glaring eyes and bony fingers' bit her throat. Fortunately the woman's tortured screams aroused her brothers from their sleep and they chased the vampire over the churchyard wall.

After a short convalescence abroad, in Switzerland, the family returned to the hall and all was quiet until several months later, when one night the same woman was woken by a scratching sound. As she looked at the window she saw the same ghastly face staring at her. Instantly she screamed and this alerted her brothers, who shot the creature in the leg. As they chased the vampire, they followed its trail of blood to an old mausoleum. Inside the mausoleum they were overcome by a terrible stench and discovered that all the coffins had been destroyed, the bodies they contained had been ripped apart and the remains scattered everywhere. All the coffins apart from one. The group opened the complete coffin and inside found the brown, mummified body of a man – bizarrely, they also discovered the bullet hole where they had shot its leg. They burned the body and no more was ever heard of the Croglin vampires.

Britain boasts a rich geographical association with the most famous vampire of them all – Count Dracula. Debate has raged for decades over the location that provided the inspiration for Bram Stoker's novel, with the two prime candidates being the east Yorkshire fishing village of Whitby and the village of Cruden Bay on Scotland's east coast. Whitby is sometimes called 'Dracula country', as it is where Count Dracula came ashore in the novel. Cruden Bay, meanwhile, is reputed to house the castle that inspired Bram Stoker to pen *Dracula* as he holidayed in the town.

The town of Whitby boasts an impressive Dracula tourist industry – you can buy the 'Whitby Dracula Trail' map from its tourist office and track down locations associated with three chapters in Stoker's novel. This Dracula Trail starts in the East Crescent, where Mina Murray and Lucy Western stayed, a pretty set of houses where they were holidaying until Dracula attacked the sleepwalking Lucy in St Mary's graveyard.

Across the harbour is the sandbank under Tate Hill, where the *Demeter* ship crashed – freeing Dracula, who had travelled on board in hidden crates of earth filled with his native Transylvanian soil, and escaped in the shape of a black dog. Stoker based the incident of a stranded ship on a real-life incident – a Russian schooner, the Dmitry, was wrecked on this bank during a storm in 1885.

One can retrace the steps of Dracula as he leapt up the 199 steps near the sandbank to the graveyard where he attacked Lucy. Mina also climbed these steps as she ran to save her friend. The graveyard has many tombs that inspired Stoker, including one that belonged to a suicide and which became Dracula's resting place, according to Stoker. After the novel's publication, this stone-carved coffin in the ruins of the abbey became nicknamed 'Dracula's Grave'.

Whitby has added to Stoker's legend by building its own. The Dracula Experience is a walk-through Dracula attraction, a series of scenes using sounds and electronic special effects, life-size models and live actors. On display there is a cape weighing 56 kg that was worn by Christopher Lee during his famed Hammer Films period. Elsewhere in the town, Dracula tourists can take home an assortment of souvenirs from 'Dracula country', including luxury chocolate coffins and black Dracula rock.

With an increase in 'vampire tourism', local businesses are keen to stake a claim in this burgeoning industry and every year more and more Dracula delights are added to the town.

Bats and Broomsticks is Whitby's only guest house completely dedicated to Victorian Gothic decoration. Visitors, as they enter the drive, are greeted by a life-size Dracula and, upon entering, will find a coffin propped up at the top of the stairs. With ornate gothic four poster beds, replica skull lamps, candelabra, mirrors and gothic fireplaces guarded by gargoyles and dragons, each room is a vampire's perfect luxury lair. Breakfast is served by candle light and although traditional breakfast is served there are suitable touches like skulls carved onto on the toast and Grim Reaper cutlery (naturally, a gothic soundtrack plays in the background, courtesy of bands such as The Damned and Siouxie and the Banshees). The proprietors do point out that 'normals' are more than welcome!

Even English Heritage is getting in on the act with its inaugural 'Nights of Victorian Gothic' which took place on Halloween 2009. Whilst their newest venture is not directly associated with vampires, it does celebrate the Victorian fascination with the Gothic. Indeed, it is more than vampire-friendly, judging by the hundreds of goth-attired and fang-bedecked attendees.

This three day event boasted a Victorian hangman (complete with his own set of gallows) and an undertaker recounting tales of his profession. For the first time in the Abbey's history visitors were able to wander around by night and experience the specially illuminated Abbey ruins. Actor Simon Kirk retold some classic Victorian stories, including extracts from works by Charles Dickens and Bram Stoker. The highlight of the event was a full Victorian gothic funeral procession with standard bearers, mutes, plumed horses and an ornate carriage.

'So many people in Whitby have embraced the town's gothic heritage and at the end of the year, when we've been looking at Whitby Abbey as a source of inspiration for writers and artists, this is the perfect time for us to explore the Gothic links with the Abbey, and the Victorian fascination with science, romance and death,' explains marketing manager, Nicola Bexon.

Although we think of Victorian people as being quite straight laced, Victorian literature was full of extremes – rich and emotional language, and to modern tastes what we might consider self-indulgent, melodramatic escapism and senti-mentality. An overt interest in science and pseudo-science led the Victorians to really question the nature of death for the first time, and this curiosity gave rise to classic works looking at both the grief of those left behind, and the possible return of lost souls in classic gothic literature. The haunting ruins of Whitby Abbey make an appearance in several book of this time, including, of course, Bram Stoker's *Dracula*.'

By comparison, Cruden Bay has been slow to fulfil the potential of its *Dracula* connections. Slains Castle at Cruden Bay is certainly fit for a Count, a roofless ruin and remains of a sixteenth century fortress sitting on a clifftop. Over a 17-year period Bram Stoker spent holidays in the small fishing hamlet of Whinnyfold, near Cruden Bay, and a short distance from Slains Castle. Slains is the ancestral home of the Earl of Eroll, and currently owned by William Elrick, of New Deer. In 1895 Stoker visited the castle as a guest of the Eroll family, and early drafts of his horror classic show Count Dracula coming ashore at Cruden Bay, which reflects that Stoker wrote at least part of his horror classic here.

The castle has been in a worsening state of repair since the roof was stripped off in 1925, but this only seemed to add to its sinister appeal. Indeed, when plans to halt the deterioration and restore the castle were announced in 2002, there was a public outcry.

The Slains Partnership lodged plans for outline planning permission to convert the site into 35 apartments, but tour operators and residents feared the proposals would deprive the area's most creepy attraction and rob the ruin of its rugged beauty. One tour company, Caledonian Heritage Tours, were horror-struck by the proposals. Managing Director John Begg who had organised former Soviet president Mikhail Gorbachev's visit to Scotland, explained: 'At the moment Slains Castle at dusk is a blood-curdling experience and you can easily imagine the impact it had on Bram Stoker's masterpiece. When we take visitors on coastal tours of the north-east the ruin of Slains is a must-see. These plans would ruin the beauty and mystery of the castle. I just cannot imagine holiday homes inside the castle ruins and hopefully it will never happen.'

Unfortunately, in 2007 Slains Castle was closed to the public due to safety risks, which was effectively the first time that the general public were not allowed access to this historic site. The cliff-top fortress was no stranger to danger, being situated at the top of a very steep cliff. Whilst it never boasted the greatest access and was not accessible to wheelchair users and prams, at least some visitors could walk around the castle. Sadly for Slains Castle it is now a battle against time, as it has been estimated that in twenty years the castle will start to crumble into the sea, along with its connection with the greatest horror novel in English literature.

Aside from these sites associated with literary vampires, and the locations for the sightings of 'real' vampires, which have already been discussed, the most famous of locations allegedly associated with vampires is London's most famous burial ground, Highgate Cemetery, which was opened in 1839 and was the burial place of choice for many during Victoria's reign. In 1967, 70 years after Bram Stoker's novel was published, stories began to circulate that a real vampire lived in the catacombs of Highgate Cemetery. Newspapers reported that a 'hideous entity' had been seen stalking the area. It was suggested that animals had been found drained of blood and that several young girls had been attacked by the creature. A tall, dark figure had been spotted by several people in the cemetery in 1969 and David Farrant, an occultist, claimed to have witnessed the spectre on several occasions as he walked by the cemetery gates. Soon other people made claims that they too had seen the vampire, and even that they had been attacked.

The drama further increased after Sean Manchester, who claimed to be an expert in vampire matters, stated that the entity was an undead European nobleman who had arrived in Highgate in the 18th century. Manchester claimed that a local girl, named Elizabeth, had fallen under the vampire's sway and that only he could save her. He therefore set out to find the vampire and stake it through the heart. However, things began to spiral out of control: foxes were discovered dead, drained of blood; bodies were pulled from their coffins and staked, their heads often missing. Manchester's claims set off a hysterical reaction: graves were smashed and bodies exhumed. A mummified corpse was found in a man's car outside the cemetery gates. The headless and charred corpse of a woman was found outside a vault by three schoolgirls in broad daylight. The normally quiet suburb had become gripped by the drama as the satanic rituals increased. Finally, when a female corpse was found exhumed, with her head removed, the police stopped any further public access to the cemetery.

Events came to a head on 14 March 1970, when vigilantes thronged the cemetery for a mass vampire hunt. Scenes of chaos ensued, but a strong police presence restrained most of the baying crowd. Manchester claimed to have located the vampire in a vault, and also claimed to have impaled the 'king vampire' in its lair.

Over the next few years, hauntings were reported, exorcisms were performed and two witnesses claimed to have been attacked by an eight-foot tall horror in the graveyard. More animal corpses were found. Eventually, the hunters claimed to have found and staked the creature and that it had been destroyed, and interest in the case waned. A few years later, however, new reports of incidents around the cemetery started up. The hunters moved in, claiming that this was evidence of a new vampire, the spawn of the first creatures in the area. They hunters eventually claimed to have killed this beast too, which they stated had taken the form of a huge spider.

In 1974, David Farrant was arrested for offences including 'offering indignity to the dead'. Manchester has since published more material on the Highgate vampire case and is still adamant that he personally killed two vampires. After his release from prison, Farrant lived in relative anonymity.

His book Beyond the Highgate Vampire tells his side of the story. In 1997 he formed the Highgate Vampire Society, whose magazine *Suspended in Dusk* continues to analyse the story. Farrant claims many revelations are yet to be made public, maintains that he was innocent of all charges and argues that the entity that plagued Highgate Cemetery may well still be active. Over 30 years later, and despite claims to the contrary, the mystery of the Highgate vampire is still to be fully resolved.

CHAPTER 5

BLOODTHIRSTY KILLERS – VAMPIRE KILLERS OF OUR TIMES

In recent decades, vampirism has occasionally taken its place within the field of criminal psychiatry. The following chapter includes accounts of serious crimes of a vampiric nature or theme. The first part highlights vampire-related murders; the latter part details vampire crimes in which murder did not take place.

THE GERMAN VAMPIRE KILLERS – TRAINED IN THE UK

Although the following murder took place in Germany, and was committed by two German nationals, it is significant because the killers claimed they had learned vampirism in the UK.

In 1995, at the age of 16, Manuela Ruda ran away from school to Edinburgh. She then moved to the Highlands, where she worked in a hotel bar in Skye. During this time she made several visits to the island's most famous resident The Leopard Man – Tom Leppard. Now a pensioner, Leppard lives as a hermit in a cave built on the foundations of a croft in a remote part of Skye. He is tattooed head to foot with a leopardskin design, and has a set of custom-made fangs. During the same holiday, Manuela moved to Islington in north London, where she claimed she met other vampires and Satanists. She also attended vampire 'bite parties', where blood drinking took place, and claimed she drank blood from volunteers, willing donors whom she had met on the internet and with whom she would visit woods and cemeteries in the London area. Attention turned on the north London district, causing the *Islington Gazette* to announce that a 'secret colony of "vampires" is operating within Islington's bars and nightclubs'. Suspicion fell on Islington's popular Slimelight Goth club.

When she arrived back in Germany, Manuela had her canine teeth removed and animal fangs fitted – 'to bite better with', she claimed. In 1999, she met Daniel Ruda through the lonely-hearts column in a German publication. Daniel had advertised himself as a 'raven-black vampire seeking a princess of darkness who hates everyone and everything'. Two years later they married.

Together with her new husband, Manuela returned to Scotland in 1999. Manuela later claimed that back in Edinburgh she found Satanists who were 'desperate to let her at their veins'. She said that men were constantly after her and she made them pay for their affections with their blood – 'That's all I wanted from them,' she insisted, 'to drink their blood. I tolerated them. They were my blood donors.' She also revealed that it was in Edinburgh that she learned to file her teeth to razor-sharp points. She said she was taught by vampires to drink blood and which veins to bite from, so that she could avoid hitting an artery. She also claimed she had slept on graves and once was even buried in a grave to see what it felt like, but did not like it as she could not breathe properly. The couple claimed to have wandered through woodland with vampires they met in Edinburgh. The time they spent in the UK clearly influenced their future vampire crimes – for Manuela admitted she got a taste for vampirism and the occult while in London and Scotland.

On 6 July 2001, Daniel (then 26) and Manuela (23) lured their victim, Daniel's work mate Frank Haagen, to their flat by saying they were having a party there. Once Haagen was inside, Daniel struck his victim on the head twice with a hammer. Manuela shouted at her husband 'Stab him in the heart' and when he complied Manuela claimed she saw a light flickering around the body and she took this to be a sign that Haagen's soul was 'going down'. The couple stabbed him 66 times before praying to Satan together. They then cut a pentagram on the dead man's stomach and drank his blood from a bowl on an altar of skulls. Afterwards, the couple had sex in an oak coffin in which Manuela usually slept.

The self-proclaimed vampire Satanists – Manuela later stated that she had sold her soul to the Devil – claimed they were acting on the Devil's orders by sacrificing a human to him. It later emerged that in their quest to be vampires they had sacrificed goats and chickens in woodland near their home before progressing to human prey.

The victim's mutilated and partially decomposed body was later found by police next to the coffin in the couple's living room with a scalpel protruding from his stomach. A death list found in the flat contained the names of future victims. The couple were arrested in their flat, the walls of which were covered in satanic slogans and hung with an arsenal of knives, axes and machetes.

During the trial Manuela appeared in full Gothic gear, her head partly shaved to reveal an upside-down crucifix and a target tattooed on her skull. She told the court: 'It was not murder. We are not murderers. It was the execution of an order. Satan ordered us to. We had to comply. It was not something bad. It simply had to be. We wanted to make sure that the victim suffered well.'

German police said any evidence pointing to possible crimes or an illegal Satanic ring in Britain would be sent to the relevant authorities. But no vampire covens came forward – indeed, the high media profile of the Ruda case would have ensured that any vampire covens maintained an even lower profile than before. Journalists had an nigh-on impossible task trying to find vampires from Edinburgh who would come forward to face the revulsion of the world press and public.

The *Edinburgh Evening News* successfully tracked down a local vampire willing to speak out, but not identified. 'Debbie' a 26-year-old retail manager in the city centre who had had her teeth capped with fangs, described how a love of vampires led her to blood drinking with her partner. She had first developed a taste for blood when she accidentally cut her tongue and while she was telling her boyfriend about her new craving he offered her some of his blood to drink. Despite her blood lust the girl did not believe that drinking blood bestowed any supernatural powers on her; nor did she believe it would give her eternal life. The newspaper also spoke to a member of an underground Goth club who refused to be identified but revealed that he knew a real vampire in Edinburgh. According to him, this vampire only surfaced at night, to drink blood.

Certainly Edinburgh's gory past and multitude of ghost tours provides a rich background for tales of vampires to survive. But the secrets that the Rudas learned in this city are still to be fully brought to light.

MABEL LEYSHON, THE 90-YEAR-OLD
VICTIM OF A VAMPIRE

On 25 November 2001, 17-year-old Matthew Hardman, who had lived just a few yards away from his victim, broke into the Mabel Leyshon's bungalow by throwing a slab through her back door window while she was watching television. He attacked the very deaf widow with poor eyesight from behind, stabbing her a total of 22 times. He then sliced her chest and made a deep gash that was almost eight inches long and nine inches wide. He opened her chest and pulled her heart out, wrapped it in newspaper, put it in a saucepan and covered it with a silver platter. Hardman then made several deep gashes along the victim's legs to drain blood. (The pan bore a tide-mark and lip print on the rim, which was evidence that Hardman had drunk from it.) He then placed two pokers arranged in the shape of a crucifix at the woman's feet and left candlesticks next to her body.

The brutal murder shocked the small, close-knit community of Llanfairpwll, on the Isle of Anglesey, a peaceful holiday town. 'The injuries are the worst I have seen in my career,' Detective Superintendent Alan Jones told reporters after the murder. The crime was featured on BBC's *Crimewatch* programme in December 2001 and police received over two hundred calls as a result. Hardman was arrested in January 2002.

When police arrived on the scene, they discovered that the newspaper that the heart had been wrapped in was not totally saturated with blood, indicating that it had had time to dry out. Hardman believed the ritual he had performed would make him immortal, as prosecutor Roger Thomas later explained: 'We submit that in November 2001 he was fascinated by and believed in vampires. He believed they existed, believed they drank human blood and believed most importantly that they could achieve immortality – and he wanted to be immortal.'

When police searched Hardman's bedroom, they found books, magazines and internet material devoted to vampires and how to become one. Books found included Bram Stoker's *Dracula*, and a library book entitled *The Devil: An Autobiography*. Examination of Hardman's computer showed that he had logged on to websites including those of the Vampire Rights Movement and the Vampire/Donor Alliance. The latter is a support group that serves the whole vampire community, and its site states: 'The site exists to serve all who might be part of vampire community: Gothic lifestyle vampires and non-lifestyle vampires alike, energy feeders, sanguinarians (drinkers of blood); succubus/incubus type vampires (sex feeders); donors, would-be donors, and other loved ones; and those who are simply curious, provided they wish us well.' Although the Vampire/Donor Alliance purports to cater for all these types of vampire, the site does admit that it is primarily concerned with blood drinkers, as the webmaster explains:

> This site has a bit of a bias toward blood feeding, because I happen to feed on blood and because there needs to be a site which hypes sanguinary safety. It's quite possible to feed without feeding on blood, but in my opinion, blood is the most efficient way of getting the life energy that we need. 'The blood is the life.' Blood carries a great deal of life force. So a

vampire is a person who needs to feed on life energy, and frequently (though not always) finds him- or herself craving blood.

In court, evidence of an incident was revealed that foretold Hardman's dangerous obsession with vampires. Two months before the murder, during a conversation with a teenage German girl student on an exchange visit to Llanfairpwll, Hardman told her the town was 'a perfect place for vampires', as there were many old people there – if any of them died after being bitten, it would be assumed that they had suffered a heart attack. In any case, he surmised, there were so many old people in the town, that no one would notice one missing. After they both spoke about Gothic fashions, vampires and the paranormal, Hardman accused the 16-year-old German girl of being a vampire. He begged her to bite his neck so that he too could become one. When she refused, he became violent and pressed his neck against her mouth.

Hardman was found guilty of murder at Mold Crown Court in August 2002 and sentenced to life imprisonment. The murder signalled the beginning of the end for vampire fans and societies. No longer were vampire murders associated with cults overseas. They had arrived in the UK.

THE QUEEN OF THE DAMNED KILLER

The first vampire murder in Scotland happened on 11 December 2002, in Fauldhouse, West Lothian. Allan Menzies murdered his friend Thomas McKendrick at Menzies' home and then buried the body in a shallow grave, which was discovered five weeks later.

The 22-year old Menzies confessed during his trial that he had killed his friend on the instructions of 'The Queen of the

Damned', and in order to become immortal as a vampire. Menzies was obsessed with the vampire film *Queen of the Damned* and had watched it more than a hundred times. He would arise at 5am, watch it, then let it play for the rest of the day. At his trial, he stated: 'I would go to bed and could never get the thought of being a vampire out of my mind. I was addicted to watching it.' Menzies claimed that Akasha, the heroine of the film, had constantly repeated her instructions to kill and she promised him immortality in return for 'souls'. 'I thought if there really is a God, I'd sacrifice this life for the next,' he revealed. 'This life is short, I'm 21, nae future, so I figured I'd sell my soul for this life to be reborn in the next.'

Menzies believed that if he murdered he would be rewarded in the next life with immortality and would return as a vampire. And the more people he killed, the more it would please Akasha, 'The Queen of the Damned'. In Menzies' mind, therefore, it was essential he committed murder, as this was the only way he could become a vampire. One evening, when his friend McKendrick asked him, 'You don't really believe in vampires or something do you?', Menzies took it as an insult and, in is own words, 'went nuts', attacking McKendrick with a Bowie knife, a kitchen knife and a hammer. His victim died after receiving at least six heavy blows to the head and 42 stab wounds to his body. Menzies confessed to pushing a Bowie knife through McKendrick's throat and into his brain.

Menzies then proceeded to drink his victim's blood and eat parts of his head. After drinking two cups of blood, Menzies went to look in a mirror to make sure his teeth were covered with blood. He then put the body into a wheelie bin before burying it in woodland.

Menzies was later jailed for life. He admitted that by the

time he committed the murder he had been buying ox liver and eating it raw, and even drinking the blood from the organ just for the sake of it. After the murder he believed he was a vampire and that he had achieved immortality. Menzies had attempted suicide after the killing, but he said that was 'to get to the next life quicker ... that's when I will be rewarded'.

James Hendry, the consultant psychiatrist for the case, had concluded that Menzies had 'a vivid fantasy life but was not mentally ill'. He said Menzies had had an abnormal personality from childhood. In Menzies' home, police had found Anne Rice's novel *Blood and Gold* from 'The Vampire Chronicles', and also hand-written notes by Menzies that read: 'The blood is the life. I have drank the blood and it shall be mine. I have seen the horror.' Police also found a cutting from *True Crime* magazine that featured the headline 'Satanic Slaughter'.

While Menzies was in prison he said he had seen Akasha in his room at the Carstairs State Hospital and that she had told him to kill again. Menzies admitted both he and Akasha were disappointed that there were no other vampires in prison with him. Just over a year after his sentence began, he committed suicide in prison.

The following is a list of recorded crimes of a vampire nature or theme. While all are serious incidents, no deaths occurred and the victims all survived.

THE BIRMINGHAM VAMPIRE

Terror struck the streets of Birmingham over Christmas 2004, when rumours spread of a crazed vampire stalking the city and biting people. Local newspapers were swamped by stories of the vampire. Some victims claimed to have been bitten after answering their front doors. On one occasion, the vampire bit three members of a family. He also bit a man walking along the street, then pounced on neighbours who came to the injured man's aid. One woman is said to have had a 'chunk' bitten out of her hand by the attacker. Initially, West Midlands police had dismissed the reports as 'urban myth', as no victims of biting attacks had come forward. In February 2005, however, a man was finally arrested and accused of biting three people. He was released on bail. So far no new confirmed incidents have been reported.

THE EXETER VAMPIRE

A similar attack to the one described above took place in Exeter, where a 19-year-old university student was bitten on both sides of her neck by a 'vampire' dressed in a black dinner jacket.

She described her ordeal as 'horrible' and became too afraid to venture out alone or sleep in her own room. Indeed she was so afraid her attacker might strike again that she moved flat. The girl, who understandably wanted to remain anonymous, had been at the Freshers' Ball in the University's Great Hall when she was first approached by the man she would later recognise as the vampire. He had tried to kiss her but she succeeded in pushing him away. Later, he came up to her again and bit her on the left side of the neck in a vampire-like attack. Despite fending him off, the man bit her again on the other side of her neck before walking away. Luckily, paramedics were present at the ball and treated her painful bite marks. Although the skin was not broken there were distinct marks left on her neck. Her attacker had told the girl he had been following her the whole night, leaving the girl fearful that he would track her down and attack her again.

The vampire was not caught by the police and so, perhaps, remains at large.

THE VAMPIRE VERSUS THE VICAR

In October 2003, self-styled vampires Benn Lewis and Scott Bower became the first people in Britain to be imprisoned for harassing a Christian – the Reverend Christopher Rowberry – at his church, St Mary The Virgin, in Eling Hill, Totton. Lewis (aged 25), a hotel porter, and unemployed Bower (26) were alleged to have made dozens of abusive phone calls to the vicar, let off fireworks outside his home, howled like werewolves at him and left obscene pictures, including one of a disembowelled Christ, on a church notice board.

Lewis told a jury at Southampton Crown Court that he was a reincarnated vampire and drank blood to see what it would do for him – specifically in the hope that it would give him strength. He remarked: 'I read in the Bible that blood is the life.'

When asked to confirm if he was indeed a reincarnated vampire, Lewis scorned the 'silly film stuff about crosses and garlic' but admitted he was a psychic vampire who absorbed energy from other people. He denied he was a Satanist and instead identified with the Lord Jesus Christ, because he too was an outcast. But he shunned Christianity, confessing 'I spit on Christian beliefs.' Lewis admitted he was interested in spiritualism and enjoyed visiting graveyards in Hampshire.

In a raid on his house police found photos of Lewis and Bower cutting themselves and drinking each other's blood – photos that Lewis admitted had been real, although other photos were found to have been staged. Police also found an article titled 'Crimson', which Lewis had written for an occult magazine. In it he commented: 'I had great trouble with most mortals because I am beyond their earthly understanding. To them I am a curse, an omen, a lost soul, a freak and all because I believe myself to be a reincarnated vampire ... My soul can never die and the flame within my spirit cannot extinguish ...

I am beyond any mortal and I can offer any fantasy, but humans are too blind with envy to see.'

Despite the seriousness of the crimes, there were several instances where Lewis's replies prompted laughter in the court. On one occasion, when Lewis was asked if he slept in churchyards and rose from graves at night, he retorted that he slept in a bed.

Lewis was jailed for twelve months and Bower for six months.

THE DRACULA MASK SEX ATTACKER

A sex attacker who wore a Dracula mask while attacking his victims struck six times in eight months in 2000. He preyed on women and girls as young as 11 in the Hayling Island and Portsmouth areas of Hampshire. The first assault happened on 1 December 1999, when an 11-year-old girl was grabbed as she cycled along a disused railway line but managed to struggle free from her assailant. In February 2000 a woman fought free from an attacker in a Halloween mask and four days later another woman was attacked by a man wearing a Dracula mask and wig with fangs dripping with fake blood, in a subway under the A27.

The attacker threatened to kill a 13-year-old girl in the churchyard of St Mary's Church on Hayling Island and in another incident he grabbed a 15-year-old girl as she cycled along a disused railway line on Hayling Island in Hampshire. The man threatened to kill her but she managed to struggle free as he tried to drag her into some bushes. The Dracula mask, which was found thrown on the ground after one of the attacks, was traced to a local shop; detectives described it as 'terrifying'.

Following a mass DNA-screening programme of men living in the area, a 51-year-old local man was later arrested.

THE VAMPIRE RAPIST

In January 2004, a man drank a woman's blood during a nine-hour attack in which he assaulted her with a glass bottle and wooden chair and raped her. The woman suffered over 60 injuries from the attack. During the attack the man ordered the woman to cut her finger with a razor so he could drink her blood, telling her: 'Now you're in my veins and this is for life.'

Luke Weekes, a 21-year-old musician, had cornered the 27-year-old woman in a hostel's dining room, grabbing her hand and telling her that he would break her fingers if she did not strip and perform a sex act on him. When she refused, he held her captive for four hours before escorting her up to his room and raping her. The terrified woman was told during the assault that if she made any noise he would kill both her and her daughter. After the assault Weekes took his victim to hospital to stop her reporting him to the police. He told hospital staff that he had rescued her after she had fallen downstairs. It was only when doctors ordered Weekes out of the examination room that the victim confessed the truth. He was jailed for 12 years.

THE INTERNET VAMPIRE STALKER

Father-of-two James Wiles from Charlotte, North Carolina, exploited a teenage girl's fascination with vampires via the internet before travelling almost 4,000 miles to England to abduct and assault her and encourage her to drink his blood.

Wiles, 43, had met the teenager in an internet chatroom, where they swapped daily emails, describing their interests in 'the darker side of Gothic, and vampirism' including self-mutilation. He began bombarding the girl with emails, text messages and phone calls in which they would discuss their shared interest in the Gothic. Wiles knew the girl was only 15, but he himself did not reveal his age, and the girl assumed he was not over 25. In early 2004 Wiles told the girl he was planning to come to England, but her parents found the emails and contacted Wiles, warning him of their daughter's age and that they would contact the police if he appeared. Wiles replied he would not travel to meet her after all.

But on 2 February 2004 Wiles telephoned the girl and told her he was outside her home. After they met, he called her school, impersonated her father and excused her absence from school that day because she had a headache. He then took her to a hotel in Norwich, where he assaulted her. Wiles asked the schoolgirl to cut him on the shoulder, and when this bled he invited her to drink his blood, which she did. He did not want to cut the girl, however, as he did not wish to leave a mark on her. Later that evening he returned her home.

The next day he returned and again telephoned the school to excuse the girl's absence before taking her to another Norwich hotel, where he assaulted her again. After this incident, the girl told her parents about her ordeal and they contacted the police.

In a police interview, Wiles claimed that he believed the girl was 17 or 18. He also denied the scar on his shoulder had been made when she drank his blood and said something had fallen on him, causing the injury. He appeared at Norwich Crown Court on 12 December 2004, and changed his plea to guilty after a transatlantic partnership between Norfolk police and US police revealed the emails from the girl's parents warning Wiles of her age. Wiles was jailed for two years and his name placed on the sex offenders' register for life.

A VAMPIRE SEX CULT

A front-page headline in the *News of the World* on 17 November 1996, screamed: 'Vampire Sex Cult Preys on Virgins'. The article exposed a vampire sex cult in Dorset that indulged in blood drinking and Satanic sacrifice. Its leader was a Satanist high priest who boasted that he had sex with young virgins in graveyards. The man had adopted the name of an ancient Transylvanian called Vandari, who was the founder of a Carpathian religion. He also claimed he was over 300 years old. Vandari and his followers would meet at their secret altar hidden in the ruins of the 15th-century Sandfoot Castle. It was here that he and his vampire disciples, known as The Family, would sacrifice chickens to a vampire god called Nosferatu. Vandari claimed he had recruited over 80 members to his cult.

During vampire rituals, Vandari would slash his chest with a razor blade and force girls to drink blood from the cut. In another ritual he would order two of his disciples to drink from the veins on his outstretched arms. He performed these rituals every month claiming the blood drinking gave him strength. Alarmingly, some members had signed a death pact willing to sacrifice their life for The Family when the time came. Vandari had told his followers that if they gave their lives to him he would be able to fly like a vampire.

Vampires who kill or commit criminal attacks are unwelcome within the vampire community. In effect, such vampires should be viewed within a criminalistic context rather than a vampire one. It is significant that practically all the vampires who killed have been institutionalized and are not welcome within the vampire community nor the general community at large.

CHAPTER 6

BLOOD LUST – END OF THE ONE NIGHT BITES. HOW AIDS KILLED THE VAMPIRE

'The blood is the life.'

So says Dracula in Bram Stoker's immortal novel. The human body needs blood to function. It is part of our life force and without it we would die. For many vampires too, blood is not only part of their life force but also of their daily feeding needs.

Ask anyone what determines a real vampire and the answer will always be the same. Blood. Common consensus demands that real vampires drink blood and this one prerequisite denotes the existence and reality of a vampire. Whether an individual drinks blood to satisfy a physical or psychological craving, the fact remains the same: vampires need blood to survive.

The modern vampire phenomenon, in the form of the sanguine vampire, was first brought to the world's attention significantly in Carol Page's book *Blood Lust: Conversations with Real Vampires* published in the USA in 1991 (the book was published in the UK in 1993). For the first time, Page delivered an in-depth study of modern-day vampires. 'They love the night, they drink blood; they want to meet you...' she wrote. 'Real vampires do exist and blood lust tells their complete, shocking story. On screen from Bela Lugosi to Gary Oldman, the Dracula myth has fascinated millions. Some people, though, feel compelled to live out their dark fantasies and actually become vampires themselves.' The author interviewed contemporary vampires, including one woman who believed that blood-drinking cures her anaemia and keeps her young – if she cannot find a donor she gnaws her own arm. Another vampire describes the taste of blood as 'the best in the world'. Fear of AIDS proves little deterrent, though one vampire interviewed in Page's book claims to abstain from 'one night bites'.

The sanguine vampire is an isolated figure, and in truth this is the curse of being a 'real' vampire in the 21st century. In the UK, blood drinking, or 'feeding' as its practitioners call it, remains a secretive and taboo subject. As a result, it is a very difficult task conducting any proper research in this area. Blood drinkers exist outside vampire societies and fan clubs, keeping themselves out of the public eye. They know only too well the dangers they face – they are perceived as a danger to society and take their place among the rank of serial killers and the psychotically deranged. No wonder they prefer to hide behind the safety of their PO box numbers and assumed names such as 'Dark Angel' and 'Lestat'. Society denies them a voice and sees them as mentally imbalanced. Rarely do they have the chance to explain that they are – except on the rarest occasions – not a danger to society. These so-called 'crazed psychotics' either drink their own blood or feed only from willing donors. And they abhor violence too.

One main difference between the blood-drinking vampire of

the cinema and its real-life counterpart is that vampires today rarely go around attacking strangers. The sanguine vampire usually has a willing donor, and develops a relationship with that donor. This can be an equal partnership, in which the vampire receives blood from the donor and the donor in return receives companionship and 'great sex', according to many donors' experience. Vampires are usually highly sexual creatures and can even satisfy their needs from sexual energy. On the other hand, those who follow the predatory vampire role find that they have crossed the boundary into sociopathology, which results in prosecution or institutionalisation.

Sanguine vampires in the UK are a reticent lot compared to their American counterparts. They are almost exclusively to be found on the safe haven of the online world, and rarely reveal their identities and habits to the real world. Sanguines are media shy in general, and television and media productions strive to find willing volunteers for projects concerning blood-drinking vampires. Often, sanguine vampires have no alternative but to go abroad to guarantee their anonymity.

Kate from Surrey, whom we heard from in an earlier chapter, believes she has all the symptoms of a vampire: she is sensitive to daylight and craves raw meat. She believes she is a real vampire and has advertised on websites for willing donors. Yet vampires like Kate are isolated not just from society itself but also from vampire societies. It is hardly surprising, therefore, that blood drinkers have been forced to retreat into their own virtual reality. They seek advice anonymously on the worldwide web, and they hide behind vampiric pseudonyms. The media ridicule them, society scorns them and vampire societies ban them. Isolated from society, many sanguine vampires are forced to seek advice from vampire 'experts' like psychic vampire and agony aunt Katharina Katt. In one letter, a worried vampire told her:

> Dear Vampire, Last night I let one of my good friends sleep over and we exchanged blood to each other but the thing I'm upset about is that when we both went to sleep I guess she decided that she was still thirsty so she cut my neck when I was asleep. When I woke up there was blood all over the pillow. I mean, it's not a big deal, I just think that it was wrong.

Katt replied:

> Dear Drained, cutting someone as well as feeding from them without permission is a HUGE no-no. If she wanted more then she should have asked, and cutting anyone on the neck is also a no-no. Some major veins are located there and you could have easily bled to death. You should seriously consider your relationship with this friend since there are some serious boundaries this person has crossed.

Sanguine vampires have their feet firmly in the 21st century and are aware of modern risks – such as AIDS. Hence, most sanguine vampire websites contain essays about safe feeding techniques and in all cases do not recommend drinking from strangers. They also advise screenings for HIV and other diseases before any type of blood play or blood exchange. Although medical knowledge insists the HIV virus is killed by stomach acids, the virus can be contracted through cuts or sores in the mouth. Sanguine vampires seem to be a sensible lot. In fact, it is a reality far removed from the media frenzy that results whenever a blood drinker is brought to the public's attention, when blood drinking becomes synonymous with depraved acts of violence and a danger to society.

Although the stereotypical vampire lunges for its victim's neck to feed, in reality this is rarely practised. Biting is not a method used by most sanguine vampires – primarily because there are easier ways to draw blood and it is illegal. Neither do vampires drink gallons of blood a day. Some drink only a few drops every couple of weeks. One vampire has commented: 'Too much blood makes you throw up. Some people cannot stomach it – they mix it with vodka or orange juice. It tastes different depending on what you have eaten. Sometimes it's nice and sweet.'

Some sanguinarians love specific blood types – instead of 'What's your star sign?' they ask 'What's your blood type?' It has also been reported that blood tastes better before it hits the air, which could explain why some vampires like to use syringes to remove the blood instead of cutting. Some sanguine vampires insist certain blood types taste better than others. Human blood is not rich and thick and nauseating when fresh from a cut, but thin and sweet-tasting. Blood is best consumed hot or warm, not chilled or at room temperature, and it must always be fresh. One sanguine vampire has commented, 'The blood of a devout Christian can taste very rewarding.'

Advice is freely available on vampire websites. 'This is one way to approach safe blood play. Some need just a few drops every few days to a week while others need more of it and more often. Blood is a natural emetic and too much of it will cause one to vomit. Some take the blood in small cups and mix with a red wine.'

Another myth to be laid to rest about sanguine vampires is

Above: Bella (played by Kristen Stewart) and her vampire boyfriend, Edward (Robert Pattinson) in a scene from the *Twilight* movies. ©WENN

Below: The love triangle, involving Edward, Bella and Jacob (played by Taylor Lautner, pictured here with Kristen Stewart), is a key feature of *The Twilight Saga*. ©WENN

Above: The London Vampire Group in Transylvania 2004.

Below left: Zachary Hunt is a lifestyler who models his look on the Gary Oldman portrayal of Dracula in *Bram Stoker's Dracula*.

Below right: Shade is a vampire lifestyler who follows the cyber tradition and bases his look on a cross between a courtly gentleman and a cyborg.

Above left: Dark Angel from The Vampyre Connexion.

Above right: The Vampyre Master.

Left: A flyer for a Vampyre Society gathering.

A few of the characters who have attended vampire and gothic events over the years, and have posed for *Bite Me* magazine. Although they are not vampires themselves, the influence on their style is unmistakeable!

© *Anita Russo*

'The Beautiful Deadly Children' are the UK vampire scene's most decadently dressed individuals.

Above left: Maximilian 'Max' Schreck, the German actor who starred in the 1922 classic *Nosferatu*.

Above right: Hungarian actor Bela Lugosi, in Universal Studios' *Dracula* (1931).

Below left: Christopher Lee in the classic Hammer Horror *Dracula* (1958).

Below right: In 1998, Francis Ford Coppola offered up his version, *Bram Stoker's Dracula*. It had an all-star cast, with Gary Oldman playing the title role (pictured here with Winona Ryder).

Above: Author Arlene Russo sits in the 'Bram Stoker Seat' looking across at the same view as Lucy and Mina, characters in Bram Stoker's novel *Dracula*.

Below left: Whitby Abbey where Dracula attacked sleepwalking Lucy in the graveyard of St Mary's graveyard in Bram Stoker's novel.

Below right: Dracula tourists can take home an assortment of souvenirs from Whitby (Dracula country), including luxury chocolates and black Dracula rock.

© *Anita Russo*

More Vampire literature.

that there are not that many of them in the first place. Mick of the London Vampyre Group observes:

> There is a dire shortage of blood drinkers in the UK – but enough people who say they are ageless, including myself. The blood scene is mainly the Scarlet Moon group, the Human Living Vampires and those who like to term themselves as 'psychic' vampires. There are enough of them around – dysfunctional people who waste your time to get attention. There are genuine people who say they need blood to get nutrition – for example, the Vampyre Society had a woman in Bristol who bought blood from the butcher to drink it. It must have been a fad, as the nutrition in blood is not really available to our digestive system – it makes you sick, as it contains an emetic. I don't really see this area as part of the vampire scene, as it is more connected with blood fetish.

Why do people drink blood? The most common reason is to obtain energy that they are lacking. But there are other reasons involved. Anthony, a 22-year-old Welsh student, was specifically interested in the powers he believed that blood drinking could give him – in particular, immortality. He says:

> My only reason of becoming a vampire donor is to confirm to myself whether or not this whole vampire business has been a masterpiece of gullible fantasy or whether there is something more to that can be read in an Anne Rice novel. Whether it was mere stupidity on my part to chase immortality in

this fashion. Immortality was my only interest, since mortality and old age terrify me, though I am now resolved to be dead before I have a chance to become demented – the lesser of two evils, even if I consider the possibility of my damnation.

No lifestyle vampire societies in the UK endorse blood drinking, including the London Vampyre Group who have appeared in dozens of lifestyle programmes on the television and radio. Nonetheless, over the years they have had to continuously ignore requests from the media to provide them with willing blood drinkers. They group states:

> We constantly try to make clear that a fascination with any aspect of 'the vampyre' does not necessitate the drinking of blood, and any such assumption is just trite and obvious. Our researches have led us to think that it is difficult for humans to gain any amount of nutrition from the consumption of blood, as it is a) hard to digest and b) incomplete in terms of the variety needed in a healthy diet. On the other hand we acknowledge that many humans knowingly consume blood in the form of sausage and similar products like 'black' sausage – indeed, a lot of us have no qualms about admitting eating and liking this. Some societies let blood from their animals to consume it … Masai tribesmen, who are herders of cattle, will take blood from their animals for nutritive and also ritualistic purposes. Taking blood from another animal, especially a human, implies several health hazards and precautions regarding the avoidance of disease are obvious.

We are aware that there are people who experience an erotic pleasure in sampling blood from a sexual or sensual partner and this is less the business of 'drinking someone dry' and more the pursuit of breaking taboos and experiencing symbolic and fetishistic pleasures. Since this is the business only of people who engage in such mutual pleasuring, it is not possible to condemn it, especially in a society that tolerates brutal practices like boxing and dog fighting in the name of sport. On the other hand, we categorically say that, for a person to be interested and involved in the vampire genre does not imply in any way that they need to indulge in blood drinking. Those who do carry out such private practices have asked us to protect their identities especially since the society we live in is not as tolerant of individualists as our 'protectors' would like us to think. Unnecessary exposure has led people into physical intimidation and danger and also loss of employment and livelihood.

Many vampires discover their blood lust for the first time in childhood, by accident. They cut themselves and find they are drawn to drink their blood. Often, though, they forget about the blood until years later when they are 'awakened'. One vampire explains:

I am a 44-year-old vampire and knew of my blood lust as a child, when I would hide in the closet and feed upon myself. I remember as a child of about five being in my room to relish the nourishment of my own self's blood. I was about eight when I found another kid in school who, if I gave him my lunch money, I could coax into doing small cuts and letting me have the little blood that was there. But I did not know the meaning of this, nor was I 'taught' about its rights and wrongs. I knew and sensed I had a need for blood energy and I felt good with it. Eventually my parents did see me licking the blood from my hand, but their reaction was 'he cut himself'.

My desire to psi-feed came later, as a teen. During most of my adult life as an energy feeder, I have been a blood/psychic vamp and I quenched my thirst with some blood/energy feeds a week, but found myself unconsciously psi- feeding all the time on the emotional and mental energy of anyone around my space. Now, I have one regular donor whom I feed from, from a couple of times a week to several times, depending on when she is available to me. I do not feed on the blood energy much any more, finding that my psychic abilities/feeding with sexual energy provide me enough energy I need for my strength. I am pleased about this arrangement as this donor is quite committed to me and I do not need to hunt as I once did.

I believe I have been fortunate, since I was old enough to know of the blood lust as a child. I knew I was born a vampire and so knew of my destiny early. I still live alone and would not have it any other way. As for the times I have found myself unable to feed, my life suffered from lethargy and low energy levels and I did not even get out of bed. I get an energy boast from the monthly full moon and I always look forward to this time. A human may like the taste of blood but a vampire needs the energy from it. True vampires do not stay well long without having this blood and psychic energy. That is why we have a need for it for our health.

Now, I just want to point out that I did not know anything about vampirism until later. And I had not been 'taught' in my morality upbringing that this was bad. I believe that my need for the blood energy were not something that I 'learned' from someone else's teachings to do or not do. Forty years later, I am still a vampire, but my energy needs have changed. Unlike the safe blood donors I had in the seventies, I now am very distrustful of this energy source. So now I mainly rely on my empathic abilities to psi-feed combining that with pranic energy sources, such as in sex. I have had many tell me that they 'enjoy' the blood energy, but I 'need' it, or a suitable substitute.

Sanguine vampires do have alternatives, should they have a craving but find themselves without a donor. To take the edge off blood craving, one sanguine vampire recommends clam chowder and lots of red drinks and rare steak – even though its juice is mostly water and food colouring, it has a psychosomatic effect. Vampire agony aunt Katharina Katt comments:

Most sanguinarian vampires complain of barely controllable cravings. Although 'blood donors' are preferred, there is the realistic danger of blood-transmitted diseases like AIDS. One main alternative many sanguinarians use is animal blood. Before you turn your nose up at the idea I want to point out that people have been using animal blood in cooking recipes since the time the written word began. From blood sausage to blood stew, many types and varieties are available. A butcher won't even blink at the request for fresh pig or beef blood. Search for a local butcher shop that will cater to your 'unusual' need. Simply tell them it is for your recipe and invite all your friends over to taste your newest kitchen creation. Vampires who drink animal blood insist human blood tastes better and has more pranic energy in it. They have reported no animalistic side effects when drinking animal blood. Theoretically there may be a difference in taste depending on the blood types as well.

One blood drinker advises against drinking one's own blood, and indeed there are several reasons why it is inadvisable:

If you're cutting yourself just to see, feel and taste your own blood, you really, really need to stop. I understand the impulses that might lead a living vampire to cut him or herself just to feel and see blood. I'm very familiar with the total fascination, the sense of getting high, the momentary easing of hunger that completely makes you forget that you're hurting yourself. When I was a teenager, cutting myself was just one of the dubious things I did to experience my own blood – and when my parents found out, there were consequences that didn't make me very happy. Now I realize clearly what a pointless and harmful exercise shedding your own blood is for a living vampire.

Drinking one's own blood will deprive that person of his own pranic energy and any 'high' that is perceived to be attained from the blood is imaginary and not actual. Furthermore there is the risk of injury and infection.

Another sanguine vampire has observed:

Even if you're using stainless steel surgical tools (are you?), sterilising them with every use (are you?) and sterilising your skin before you cut (are you?), there is still a significant chance of infection. Your immune system might be lower than usual; there might be disease organisms in the environment. Even hospitals can't prevent infections in their patients, so how can you? And infections can have very serious consequences, including loss of a limb by amputation, and death.

Of course, vampires differ from non-vampires in another very important area. Vampires have the added burden of their identity, the challenge of having to explain how they received their cuts or, indeed, why they are cutting themselves. Society does not yet accept vampirism as a physical condition and vampires who proclaim they are cutting themselves are likely to be questioned over their psychological state. Vampires rightly fear that cutting themselves is an act that is usually not understood by a society that views cutting oneself as an act of attempted suicide. One concerned person highlighted an even worse scenario – the vampire could find him- or herself sectioned in a psychiatric hospital: 'No one [but another living vampire] will understand or believe why you did what you did.' She continues:

> This is especially true if you don't get medical attention because you're afraid of having to explain how you got cut. Have you studied anatomy? Can you be sure that you won't sever a tendon or an artery? Veins and arteries under your skin will move around, due to scar tissue forming, if you cut in the same place more than once. Every individual has a unique body structure, and you might perfectly well have an artery where one 'isn't supposed' to be. If you sever a tendon, you may lose the use of a finger or hand permanently. When there are sharp blades involved, nothing is predictable. Pets jump on you, phones ring unexpectedly, hands slip or jerk without warning.

In an interview for *WOW! Magazine*, sanguine vampire Thia explained that she has been drinking blood since she was a child. She prefers human blood, and will only drink her own blood when 'donors' are not available. She advertises on the internet for people who will – either for cash or sexual kicks – provide blood She says:

> I don't really have a very great interest in vampire mythology. I don't want to be a white-faced, fanged person in a cape who sleeps in a coffin. I prefer to call myself a sanguinarian. I just need to drink blood. It started when I was very young – when other kids fell over in the playground, I would run after them and lick the blood off their legs. I'm

unemployed, so I can't really pay for it. I am due to meet a new donor soon, and he's a masochist, so no one loses out.

The internet offers an ideal opportunity for blood drinkers to share suggestions and offer tips to each other. One common topic concerns what sanguines should do if they are unable to obtain their regular blood supply. One sanguine offers some suggestions:

> If the hunger gets really bad I drink tomato juice and try and convince myself that it is blood or I eat black pudding. If I can't get these I lose myself in music but these are never as fulfilling as blood. Or you could drink yourself stupid on Bloody Marys, which I have done before now. I always find that cappuccino and coffee or a large McDonald's milkshake can take the edge off. Being a vegetarian I don't know much about animal blood, but I hear that liver is rather good for blood cravings and also that you can purchase ready-liquefied liver, lungs etc. from a butcher. I presume you can also purchase animal blood without the carcass too, though funny looks may be received.

Interestingly, people who suspect they are vampires with a blood habit are rarely encouraged to seek professional help on these sites. Acceptance is the key word: 'You have to accept what you are,' one site explains. 'It cannot be changed and denying it will only bring you heartache and grief. As you come to terms with what you are take the time to make friends with other vampires.'

Assuming that vampires do indeed exist, one might

question why. Inanna Arthen has written many essays on vampirism, which are often referenced in many real vampire websites. One essay titled 'What do you mean by a real vampire?' confirms:

> It is my belief that more real vampires than ever before (proportionately to the population) have been born in the second half of the 20th century. Their enhanced capability to manipulate life force is a skill that will be desperately needed in the earth changes to come. No other beings will have the healing abilities of real vampires that have trained themselves to use their power ethically. The price of this healing skill is one of the oldest trade-offs in the world, known to every culture and society: fresh blood in return for fertility, healing, growth and rebirth. But real vampires won't require their 'donors' to die. They'll use the energy released by a minimal amount of blood in the most efficient possible way.

But times were to change for sanguine vampires. In a paranoia-gripped AIDS society, the subject of blood exchange was rapidly to become taboo. During the 1980s and 1990s, dozens of vampire films were produced. Over 70 were released in 1990–1992 alone, and some commentators have suggested this output coincided with a cultural crescendo of AIDS anxiety. In an article in the *Sunday Times* dated 6 September 1992, Patrick McGrath saw significance in the slew of vampire films released that year. Noting the resurgence in popularity of vampire books and films, he wondered whether it could be linked to AIDS paranoia. With several vampire films due for release that year, including John Landis's *Innocent Blood*,

Buffy the Vampire Slayer and *Bram Stoker's Dracula*, McGrath asked:

> Why such sudden interest in these ghouls? What can account for their enduring appeal? And what does the current rash of vampires owe to AIDS? The question is not asked idly. Trailers for Coppola's film, which feature pools of blood slowly infecting one another, drive the analogy home as explicitly as one can ... The vampire cannot die, being dead already, or rather 'undead'. He is the ultimate transgressor. And he infects through the blood. In this light an analogy to AIDS is hard to miss.

Some critics have suggested that part of the reason for the popularity of Anne Rice's books is that latter-day interest in vampires arose at the same time as our awareness of AIDS. As this blood disease grew, thus fears of sex and blood were intermingled. Vampires needed blood to survive, and with AIDS in the news never before had so much attention been focused on contaminated blood. Blood-drinking vampires were accused of endangering the public health through the spread of disease, especially AIDS, and many vampire organisations were forced to put health advice on their websites. The Vampire/Donor Alliance strived to convey a similar message on their site, to allay fears that vampires were reckless in their feeding habits in light of the threat posed by this new global disease. As well as including several essays on their site about safer feeding techniques, they stated: 'Drinking from strangers is NOT recommended. On the other hand, just because we are in a high-risk group does not automatically make us icky, dirty, diseased, and tainted.'

In *V is For Vampire*, author David J. Skal asserts:

> The epidemic of AIDS gave the modern world a primitive shot of fear in the 1980s and 1990s, and the characteristic of AIDS itself weirdly echoed the classic motifs of vampire legends: a blood-borne, wasting malady appears, each victim capable of creating others through vein-puncturing. Science is baffled. Self-appointed moral guardians come forth, waving religious talismans, insisting that the affliction is the work of the devil. Nonetheless, the vampire seems unstoppable; in the streets, there is a steady procession of coffins. AIDS is the undeniable subtext of the explosive growth of vampire entertainment in all media during the last decade; to the unconscious mind, the reality of AIDS can be almost too much to bear, but on the plane of fantasy, the threat of AIDS death can be bargained with – defanged, as it were.

Vampires counteracted this by stating that sanguine vampires did not endanger the public health through the spread of diseases. They argued that they took the necessary precautions and maintained that blood-drinking posed less risk than unprotected sex. One sanguine vampire claimed: 'Blood vampires present no greater danger to the public welfare than anyone else. Blood vampires are no more interested in dying than anybody else!'

Nonetheless, HIV/AIDS did have an impact on the blood-drinking vampire community, who decided to seek other less dangerous ways to feed – something that may explain the rise of psychic vampires.

CHAPTER 7

ALL IN THE MIND –
PSYCHIC VAMPIRES
HIT BACK

I am 32 and teach physics in the UK. Long have I searched for someone who could assist me in my quest for information that would help me to realise what I feel deep in my heart. After searching for some time the only conclusion I reach is that I may be a psychic vampire. I have friends and family – they would not understand. I have a female companion, but she does not see what I see nor feel what I feel. As a physicist I have looked at things in a logical manner for much of my life but what I feel inside cannot be explained logically. I am quite lucid and would ask anyone reading this, to direct me to message boards, helpful organisations, meetings in the UK that could rest my searching soul. Be advised, what you have read here is the FIRST message that I have posted on any message board – EVER.

I have used the internet since 1995 and have never felt the need to ask anything of anyone. I am asking now. I have chosen this board to reveal myself as it was the only one I found in the UK.

Not all vampires drink blood. Some want energy instead. Meet the psychic vampires.

Psychic vampires 'feed' off another person by draining their life force via their energy. During this process the person doing the feeding comes to feel stronger, more alert, while the person being fed on begins to feel tired and exhausted. Psychic vampires lead very secretive lives, afraid of what will happen when people discover who they are and what they do. They have developed means of meeting similar people who share their cravings and can help satisfy them without drawing attention to themselves.

Katharina Katt is a psychic vampire and has been active in the vampire community for over 15 years, as well as providing advice to vampires all over the world in her capacity as a vampire agony aunt for *Bite Me* magazine. Katharina is in constant communication with many different types of vampires worldwide. She is an American who lives in Germany and travels frequently to the UK. 'I estimate there are between several thousand to several hundred thousand psychic vampires in the UK,' she says. 'The problem with psychic vampires is that many don't know what they are, or even realise that they are feeding off others.'

A psychic vampire is unable to produce the energy needed to survive for themselves. This life energy, also known as pranic energy, is naturally created by the body, and so psychic vampires have to feed off others to keep their levels of pranic energy stable. Although this energy exists in its highest form in blood, psychic vampires prefer to feed from non-blood sources. So why do psychic vampires avoid blood? Katharina Katt explains:

> Psychic vampires do not feed on blood for the same
> reason that sanguinarians do not feed on energy.

Basically they can't! Psi vampires feed on energy. They have no 'blood lust' or craving for blood. It is the same as the difference between a sheep and a lion. They are both animals, but they certainly aren't the same. Now there ARE some mixed vampires who are partly psi and partly sanguinarian, but they are usually separate. Those are the mixed breeds.

Psychic vampires believe their vampirism is not so much a medical condition as a mental ability. They claim to have heightened sensory abilities that other people lack and that they can manipulate the mental and emotional energies of others. Usually, psychic vampires become aware of their nature during adolescence. They first begin to see the energy fields and auras of people around them and then learn to manipulate their psychic energies for personal gain.

Some view psychic vampires and blood vampires as two different races. Just as a sanguinarian vampire does not usually have psychic abilities, a psychic vampire naturally possesses psychic abilities and feeds psychically because it feels natural to do so. There are often arguments between both categories of vampires, one category believing itself to be superior over the other. The Vampire/Donor Alliance refutes the common notion that sanguine vampires have more right to deem themselves true vampires than psychic vampires. In fact, many sanguine vampires believe it is a cop-out for people to call themselves vampires and then say they don't need blood. The Vampire Donor Alliance offer a different view:

There are several definitions of vampires in the dictionary, including one from the early 20th century, which refers to a sexually adventurous woman as a vampire [hence the term 'vamp']. Vampirism is used metaphorically these days to describe any sort of leeching, whether it refers to blood, money, ego strokes, or whatever. We who hunger have just as much right to call ourselves 'vampires' as modern-day Wiccans have a right to call themselves 'witches'. I do think, though, that had it not been for the popularisation of the vampire in Victorian fiction, Hollywood horror films, then later popular culture, vampirism would not be such a common metaphor, nor would self-identified 'vampires' refer to themselves as such. If we had an adjective at all, we'd probably be calling ourselves fey (touched by fate, weird, unusual, a little spooky, associated with the fairies).

Hence, there is no clear-cut classification between sanguine vampires and psychic vampires and no definitive answer to the question of whether they both belong to the same family of vampires. Since both sanguine and psychic vampires feed on essences that come from another organism, both can be considered vampires. One takes energy, another takes blood, but both need to draw on an energy source from another human to keep the life flowing through themselves. Psychic vampires claim they possess many skills and abilities, primarily increased psychic powers. Some claim they can see people's auras, sense the future and travel while they sleep. Some even claim to 'bend' other people's thoughts.

Sanguine vampires believe life energy to be strongest in blood. Bloodletting releases that force, as well as a lot of other energy. A psychic vampire can withdraw this life energy from non-blood sources. Energy can be obtained by physical actions such as touching, kissing, or biting, or by passively soaking in the ambient energy of a room or situation. Neither does the energy have to be human, as some psychic vampires 'feed' off animals or the Earth's own natural energy.

The human energy that psi vampires use is either 'latent' – the energy a human gives of in a normal state – or 'high state' emotional energy. Hence, a psychic vampire can feed without the victim knowing, something that is generally not possible for a sanguine vampire. Psychic vampires without regular donors have discovered ways to obtain an energy fix. They often stand in busy places, like pubs or train stations, and imagine the excitement of the crowd flowing into them. Others stand against a tree and feel its strength seep into them while breathing deeply. Some psychic vampires even feed off their pet cats. Katharina Katt explains: 'Energy can be absorbed from plant life, storms (usually with an amount of electricity – lightning – involved), animals and humans. This does not mean that all psi vampires are able to feed from all of these sources. Usually a psi vampire has a speciality that they are able to feed from.'

The psychic vampire should pay heed to the source of the energy and be sure not to 'kill' that source. For example, feeding on a plant continuously can destroy it. Thus, many psychic vampires avoid feeding off plants and animals, both of which contain smaller levels of energy, and therefore can become pained or die if drained too severely. Katharina Katt explains:

> Just like feeding from humans, the individual donor feels weakened and tired afterwards and needs time to recover – usually a good night's sleep is good enough. Theoretically, if an individual source is fed from constantly it will not have time to fully recover

and can become sick. It is quite normal for the psychic vampire to feed from several sources and groups of sources instead of just one on a daily basis. For example, a psychic vampire who can feed from plant life may walk through a forest or section of trees. He does not specifically draw energy from one specific tree each time, but will take a little from each one, or the radiating energy from the whole forest around him. Usually giving a source a day or two to recover, and not taking a full recharge from that source at any one time, is enough to allow the source to become healthy again.

So how much energy do vampires need? And how often do they need to feed?

Katharina Katt again:

How often a psychic vampire needs to feed depends on how much they are able to absorb and how much they are used to absorbing. Think of it as a rechargeable battery. If you only leave it in the charger for five minutes its energy will not last very long, but if it is fully charged then it can last days, or even a week! The same is true with the psychic vampire. What limits the ability of fully charging is the availability of a food source. Psychic vampires that are able to feed from nature and animals have a much more available food source than a psychic vampire who insists on only feeding from donors. Some psychic vampires are able to feed from large groups of people which can fully charge them.

However, some psychic vampires alienate themselves, becoming non-social and very closed in. The depression which comes with not feeding can lead this into a downward spiral which starves the psychic vampire and weakens them. The psychic vampire does not have a 'blood lust' that can occur when they have not fed enough and need to, so becomes lost in this downward spiral until something pulls them out of it. Specifically psychic vampires only need to feed once a month, however this leaves them starving and drained most of the time in between. Feeding weekly is ideal and feeding a small amount per day would keep them fully charged at all times. Psychic vampires have been known to go months without feeding – however, it affects both their physical and mental health quite extremely and is usually noted by physicians as antisocial and depressed behaviour.

There are many different types of psychic vampires, and they feed on different types of energies. 'Empathic' vampires feed off emotions and feelings such as anger; 'chaotic' vampires feed off situations such as fights and brawls. Some feed on positive emotions, while others prefer negative emotions. Some vampires deliberately choose donors who are excessively upset or angry and feed off their excess emotion. Although psychic vampires can feed on other people's energy from a distance, some psychic vampires who have only recently discovered their abilities feel the need to touch their 'donor' by a handshake or a light touch on the shoulder. These novice vampires can be spotted a little more easily as a result.

On the other hand, experienced psychic vampires can collect their energy over many thousands of miles and do not even need to see their donors. Many of them use internet chatrooms to do so. Katharina Katt:

> Often the emotions of a donor will taint the energy a psi vampire absorbs which can give the energy what the psi vampire would call a flavour. Just as some people like spinach and some don't, there are some emotions that some psi vampires enjoy that other psi vampires do not. However, there is a technique that some of the more experienced vampires have developed and call 'filtering'. Using filtering they separate the emotions from the energy, thus blocking out the emotions and discarding them, allowing only the pure energy to be absorbed. Once a friend came to me, and he was so angry he was shaking. He said that he needed my help to calm down again, but he feared that his anger and hate would harm me. I assured him I would filter the emotions and [told him] not to fear. He held my hands and he let it go, all the built up energy from his anger and hate flowed through him to me. I filtered the emotions, not absorbing them but just the raw energy. Afterwards he felt better and said so. He thanked me. I could tell he was still angry, but he was calmer.

Unlike sanguine vampires, psychic vampires can feed on several subjects simultaneously, by feeding off crowds. In this way, the individual subject is less likely to notice the withdrawal of energy as the vampire is only extracting very small amounts of energy from each person in the crowd. One vampire advises: 'Make sure you're focused, and feel the energy in the crowd all around you. Feel it swirl about as the mass moves. Then, WILL the energy to you. Take it in as if you were putting your head in a waterfall and letting the water rush over you.'

Alexander is a self-confessed psychic vampire. In an interview for *Bite Me* magazine he revealed his secrets:

It all began when I was really ill during my teens. Despite medication and bed rest, I just couldn't shake off this terribly exhausted feeling. I felt like I had absolutely no energy. Then one day I was sitting on the couch playing with the new puppy. This little thing was full of energy was squirming about on my lap when I suddenly felt really jealous of it – I wanted to feel like that. I became aware of this strange tingling in my hands and arms: it went all they way to my chest and I had to push the dog off my lap because I felt really dizzy. But when the dizziness had past I felt this great euphoria, for the first time in months I felt like my old self. Back then I had never heard of psychic vampirism and I didn't know that the sudden rush of energy I had experienced had come from the dog.

As I got older I noticed some strange things. I could walk into a room full of people and it was like standing in the sea with the waves washing over you. I could sense what each person was feeling. I would pick a person whose 'energy' felt good and I would go over and talk to them. I would always feel great after that. But there were times when I felt so tired and so drained that I could barely move. One day I walked into this party I'd been invited to and I could sense something strange. There was this strange buzz that

I hadn't felt before. It was like some really strong magnet pulling me into the room. I looked around and there was a dark-haired guy standing in the corner. As soon as I looked at him I knew he was the cause of the strange feeling. He was smiling at me and I just walked straight up to him and asked him who he was.

He was a psychic vampire. He knew that I was one because he had been watching me for some time, but he had been 'shielding' himself from me so that I couldn't sense him. He told me I too was a psychic vampire and explained everything. He taught me how to control the feelings, how to use my abilities and, most importantly, how to 'feed'.

Whether a vampire belongs to the sanguine or psychic variety, questions of ethics are inevitably raised. Ethics is less of a problem for blood-drinking vampires, as they are mostly involved in consensual acts of blood exchange from covens and associates. Psychic vampires, however, can obtain their energy without their victim's consent, and indeed without their knowledge.

Thankfully, the psychic vampire community tends to agree that the taking of energy without consent is a form of rape and is generally avoided. But as ethics is a matter of personal choice, one cannot ignore those who operate outside vampire communities and codes of honour. If it is a question of survival the psychic vampire will follow animal instinct and feed for survival on its prey, with the issue of ethics unlikely to come into the equation. Thus, an energy-depleted vampire will draw energy from the most convenient source, not necessarily letting ethics determine what essentially is its survival. Those who practise non-consensual feeding do not class this as rape and liken it to the survival of nature as evident in the animal kingdom. After all, it is a question of survival and if psychic vampires need to feed then they must find a way of doing so as unobtrusively as possible. This means extracting as little energy as is needed to replete the energy level, thus minimising harm. This is 'survival within reason', according to one psychic vampire.

Nonetheless, psychic vampires are often portrayed negatively – commonly as energy-seeking monsters on a mission to drain the life out of everything for their own personal gain. Katharina Katt explains:

> Most of the vampire population is not involved with 'vampire communities', but every person, vampire or not, has their own codes and ethic beliefs. It is the vampires that are young, inexperienced, and still have very little control of their abilities that are the ones – under desperate conditions – that can make rash or impulsive decisions. This could be a teenager who is desperate to feed and decides he wants someone in his class to suffer because he hates him. Thus he would feed a full charge amount from this person and weaken them. This feeding or minor attack would not be able to be proved even if the vampire admitted to it. I call it a minor attack because true psi attacks are much different and in most cases only used to protect themselves.

So how does one know if one is a psychic vampire? Many psychic vampires experience an 'awakening'. This moment of realisation can be anything from a change in mood to an event. Some warning signs that can happen to psychic vampires before they awaken include a feeling of unexplained emptiness or a strong sense of how those around you are feeling, with them often feeling tired or irritable for no reason. You may feel energy about you, see auras, and other psychic phenomena that you did not observe before. Additionally, you may discover that your sensitivity to sunlight is increased and that drinks with citric acid start to cause stomach cramps. According to the internet site Psi-Vamp, when psychic vampires 'awaken' they are often tired, depressed, and even have pains due to the increased need to absorb energy, which has a draining effect. Psi-Vamp states:

> One excellent way of determining if you're a psi-vamp is by trying to feed. If you feel a significant difference in your attitude and overall pep, you could indeed be a psychic vampire. Being a psi-vamp isn't all about seduction and secrecy. It's a difficult process of learning how to survive. You don't become immortal. You don't transform into Brad Pitt or Tom Cruise. And no, there is no Anne Rice to call you to congratulate you on your transformation. It's you and you alone.

Of course, there is the possibility that many psychic vampires are unaware of their nature and may be inadvertently feeding on others. Sometimes it takes a while for them to realise they have been unintentionally feeding on their partners and friends. Hence, it is important to study one's fluctuations in mood and energy levels. A test to confirm one's psychic vampirism would involve analysing reactions to standing near a large group of people. If the person suddenly feels more euphoric and happy, there is a possibility that that person is a psychic vampire.

In an attempt to produce the proper amount of pranic life force, psychic vampires sometimes eat large quantities of fruits and raw vegetables, as the vitamins and minerals in them help produce energy. Fruits especially recommended to combat low energy levels include strawberries, pineapple and blueberries. These fruits have high concentrations of antioxidants that help destroy free radicals, which destroy cellular make-up. High-protein foods such as meat, cheese, live-culture yoghurt, nuts, milk, soy products and peanut butter are recommended substitutes for pranic energy and are often used by sanguine vampires when they cannot find a donor. Herbal and vitamin supplements such as ginseng, vitamin B complex, and potassium can also help maintain energy levels. Bizarrely, one psychic vampire recommends 'fresh milk if you can squirt it out of the cow or goat'. And shunning vampire myth, psychic vampires add garlic to this list of recommended food energy sources.

Liquid intake is important too, and psychic vampires should keep hydrated to maintain healthy energy levels and drink a lot of water daily. They should also drink energy drinks such as Red Bull, sports drinks like Gatorade and powdered energy enhancers, available from health food shops. Psychic vampires believe that cleansing the digestive tract with dandelion and camomile helps to eliminate toxins and negative energy sources, thus allowing for proper energy flows.

Psychic vampires can develop their psychic skills so that they can counteract psychic attacks on their energy space. Katharina Katt explains:

> Psychic vampires do not usually knowingly attack people, but if the occasion arises where you've 'really pissed one off' you can use this simple technique to

protect yourself. It's call a 'shield'. Simply concentrate on your inner self and your inner light. The core of your spirit is located below your heart in your chest. Concentrate on this area and the white light there and expand the light until it's a large globe surrounding you. As long as you don't let it weaken they will not be able to get through. This technique has also worked to ward off ghosts and demons.

When a psi vampire feeds it is not usually called a 'attack'. Attacks are much more violent and harmful than a simple feeding, even if the person isn't aware they are being fed from ... Psi vampires CAN use their abilities to attack someone if they so wish – however, this is not something they commonly do or feel a need to do. It is my experience that the only times psi vampires have done it is when they have been threatened. However, I have never needed to use my 'attack' abilities. Personally, I have never experienced a 'psychic' attack, but I have been attacked by a demon before and the 'shield' is one of the first things I was taught in order to protect myself until I could be freed of the situation.

Psychic attacks can come in different types. A true attack from a psi vampire is not very common, but can come in several forms. Some can feed off the energy in great amounts, forcing the other person to weaken, but another [way] is by shocking the other person. The psi vampire has a great amount of energy stored up, especially if they feed on a daily basis. If they choose to they can emit these shocks in great blasts. Imagine a stun gun. The person receiving it is often physically pushed back and they feel the numb tingling as if they had been shot with unseen electricity. This can in no way kill someone, but is indeed a unpleasant experience. If the psi vampire is forced to use this attack repeatedly, they will quickly lose their energy because they are using the energy that they have stored for themselves. Once the battery is empty it has nothing left to give. Psi vampires reserve attacks for the primary reason that it takes a lot of energy that they could use for their daily energy needs.

One psychic vampire describes a psychic attack:

I was in a club with another vampire and we both were aware of each other. He reacted to my presence as an invasion of his territory. He walked around me and used his psychic skill to probe and disturb my energy space. I proceeded to disrupt his energy attack even further by entering his energy space. By moving my physical location about the club even nearer to his energy space, I forced him to use more of his energy and weaken him. I then proceeded to 'feed' off his energy expenditure with my own psychic ability. Energy disruption is like a cat and mouse game – you take that person's energy as a food source for yourself, thus draining the offending person. I eventually caused disruption of the other vampire's energy, causing him to leave the physical space he held and vacate the club.

I do not appreciate another vampire's attempts to psychically drain me, and I do not tolerate it. I have only found two vampires who have attempted such a psychic attack on me in the last six months. Both left the area. Those that consume successfully the emotional energy of others may be most successful with this among large groups of people such as at a music show or concert or large public events such as festivals.

Essentially, vampires are a product of their times and must therefore find ways to exist within their environment and must obtain their 'food' within that environment without being penalised for doing so. The 21st century has already seen the growth of psychic vampires who can secretly practise their beliefs and sustain their existence while living in mainstream society. Who knows what breed of vampire will flourish in the 22nd century? The next generation of psychic vampires might find that society does not view them as a threat and that they are allowed to practise their beliefs – always with consensual donors, of course – within the law. Underground communities would thus no longer be necessary, and vampirism would gain mainstream acceptance in the same way that Wicca has.

Vampires adapt to the times they live in and the next generation of vampires could find ways of feeding that have not been discovered yet. If vampires existed before mankind became civilised, it would have been easier for them to feed on blood, as self-survival instincts would have prevailed over questions of social morality. But centuries later the institution of law would not tolerate the same behaviour and thus vampires have had to evolve codes of secrecy. Vampires also adapted their feeding techniques and psychic vampires grew in force because they could find a way of obtaining life energy fairly inconspicuously and without the panic that blood-drinking causes the moral majority. A final comment from Katharina Katt:

> Theoretically, the psi vampire can feed off anything that exhibits energy in a living Ki wavelength. However, perhaps in time vampires can evolve and be able to absorb energy from electronics and non-living sources. After all, as said before, some psi vampires can feed from storms and these do not necessarily contain a living organism with Ki wavelengths. Perhaps the evolution has already begun.

CHAPTER 8

FANGS AND BLOODSHOT EYES – MEET THE VAMPIRE LIFESTYLERS

'I always thought the vampire was the most charming, magnetic monster of the whole supernatural pantheon.' (Anne Rice) Anne Rice's take on vampirism reinvented the vampire as a more romantic, sympathetic figure than had been previously seen. No longer was the vampire the stuff of nightmares. Now he was a figure to aspire to – and to dress like. When her book *Interview with the Vampire* was published in 1976 she introduced the idea of the vampire in society, inspiring the desire in many people to live the vampire life, although many chose to adopt only certain elements from it, such as the costume, and not the killing and blood-drinking. But it was really when the book was turned into a lavish blockbuster in 1992 that the vampire lifestylers came into their own. Interestingly, vampire lifestylers were generally unknown before then.

Bram Stoker's Dracula was promoted intensely by Columbia Pictures, and enjoyed the most extensive merchandising tie-ins of any film before *Jurassic Park*. This extreme media onslaught fuelled the public's imagination even more. But then, the appeal of the vampire is easy to understand. Few of us would not wish for the benefits that come with being a vampire: eternal youth, eternal beauty, power, glory, mystery, immortality, sexual irresistibility, superhuman strength and utter sophistication. In an article in the *Sunday Herald* in October 2003, Dr Glenice Byron, who teaches at the UK's only postgraduate course in Gothic Imagination at Stirling University, sums up this side of the vampire's appeal: 'It's the only monster to which society has become attached to such an extent. No one wants to go about looking like a zombie, for example. And it helps that we've also made it into a very sexy creature in recent times – you don't see anyone wanting to be the shambling vampire like the original.'

Vampire lifestylers adopt the vampire aesthetic by dressing in appropriate costume. Ladies wear traditional corsets and long velvet skirts while men wear morning suits and cloaks. The colour of the clothing is mostly the colour of blood – red and purple – though the most popular colour is always black. The traditional 'undead' look is popular – a white face and heavily black-rimmed eyes enhanced by prosthetic fangs and eerie coloured contact lenses. Blood Vial Jewellery is the latest choice for the stylish lifestyler. Each pendant is filled with special FX movie blood, but the vial can also be purchased empty and filled with perfumes, hair and ashes. Lifestylers can even fill the vial with real blood, though the manufacturers provide carefully worded advice on the matter:

'Blood can be tricky. We DO NOT RECOMMEND slicing or stabbing yourself to get a sample! Let a professional handle it! Your doctor can take a small sample and add it to the vial with a syringe with little effort. Your doctor can also add an anti-coagulant to keep the blood from clotting in the vial. Although your doctor may think this is strange, it isn't illegal. Make sure you bring the stopper and cap along with a tube of superglue to seal the vial right there in the doctor's office.

Many lifestylers decorate their homes in a dark Victorian or funeral parlour style. Rooms are draped in black velvet and popular ornaments include gargoyles and black candles. Often lifestylers are comforted by having coffins in their houses, and use them as items of furniture, perhaps as a coffee table or book case.

But it is not just a question of aesthetics. The vampire affects the wider existence of lifestylers, from the vacations they take to the red wines they drink. These people regard vampirism as a state of mind or mode of existence rather than a desire to vampirise others by feeding on them. Furthermore, it is not just outward appearances that lifestylers are attracted to. They strive to imitate the qualities of the vampire-like loyalty to others of their kind: individuality, power and elegance of style.

Lifestylers vary in their intensity of devotion to vampirism, from those who simply dress in a vampire style and who frequent vampire theme events and nightclubs to those who follow a code such as The Long Black Veil. Occasionally some lifestylers drink blood and can therefore be considered real vampires, but usually they are more interested in taking on only the appearance of vampires. This crucially differentiates them from real vampires who go beyond aesthetics of the vampire. In other words, lifestylers live the lifestyle, not the life, of the vampire.

They receive a lot of support from fellow lifestylers, and indeed society in general. Moreover, the media positively adore these vampire 'wannabees', whose elaborate costumes and elongated canines, enliven their feature pages. Lifestylers have no problems in shopping in the high street for their clothing and fangs; nor do they lack places to socialise, from horror theatre productions to Gothic nightclubs. They do not need to hide from society – rather, they like to flaunt their appearance at any media opportunity that comes their way. They value the social aspect of the vampire scene and often form their own community, though the UK lifestyler scene is a relatively small one – no more than a few hundred people at any one time.

Issue three of *Bite Me* magazine featured an interview with 'vampire lover' Jenna. She adheres to certain characteristics of a vampire lifestyle, including: Victorian-style clothing; permanent fangs; and a black-walled Gothic bedroom, including a black coffin which she sleeps in. Having overcome her initial feelings of claustrophobia, Jenna now boasts of a good night's sleep in her purple silk-lined coffin. However she points out that 'proper ventilation is essential'. One particular benefit she cites occurs in summer, when the coffin provides respite from the long daylight hours.

In the same article, another vampire lifestyler, claims that he only sleeps in his coffin three or four nights a month when he is 'in the mood', and claims to wake-up feeling refreshed and energised.

Another English lifestyler, called Shade, sums up the appeal of the vampire:

The main appeal of vampires to me has to be the whole eroticism and calculated hedonism of it all (the teeth are pretty cool too). One only has to dress in the preferred style of the vampire and a whole new personality shines through, one which people can see. This automatically draws people to you – they don't really know why, although in my opinion it is an unconscious erotic curiosity. They want to know what it would be like to be seduced by a vampire. The vampire plans vivid fantasies in lurid detail and is not afraid to enact them and this can often lead to physical and sexual excess; every part of this fantasy is planned before the event. That is not to say spontaneity is not applied, quite the opposite in fact – fits of pure emotion often drive the vampire to new heights. After all vampires are creatures of emotion, pure and lustful.

My favourite vampire films are the more modern ones – *Near Dark*, *Blade* (although it's a bit Hollywood-ised), *Bram Stoker's Dracula*, and of course *Interview with the Vampire*.

One of the best sources of vampire material, which brings the vampire into the modern era, is *Vampire: The Masquerade* by White Wolf. Although it is a role-playing game, which is not everyone's cup of tea, it is still a cornucopia of interesting ideas. Plus, it helps bring new blood into the vampire scene.

Lifestylers like Shade are aware of their own reality and hence mortality. They are under no illusions that they will live forever, and do not crave blood in an effort to achieve this end. The vampire merely provides a role they can escape into, one that gives them satisfaction. Lifestylers do not want to become vampires in the true sense, and do not indulge in any vampire criminal activities. They choose the era that appeals to them and adapt their costume to suit.

Shade uses his creativity and by his costume defines himself as a 'paradoxical anachronism'.

He continues:

The concept of being a 'traditional' vampire has always held a certain amount of eroticism, the style of dress, the mystique of a time gone by where gentlemen were true gentlemen and ladies were voluptuous and pale, a time when courtly balls were held by vastly wealthy and powerful lords. The seductive gaze of the pale count could lure the most hard-hearted mortal to his every whim.

However, times are moving onwards and change must follow – to try and keep this traditionalism is difficult, and like the herds of mortals that surround us the vampire must change. So here we have the paradox: a traditional attitude that incorporates the tides of change – the cyber tradition. Within this paradox rises a completely new breed of vampire, a new look and a new way of thought. The look becomes somewhat like a cross between a courtly gentleman and a cyborg. Shades and electronic patches with LEDs flashing perfectly complement the lace frills and velvet clothing. The thoughts change to creation of a traditional vampire through modern mediums, art may be inspired by PC software, ancient castles will be visited either by a modern mode of transport such as the car, or virtually through the world of the internet.

The world must change, it is the way of nature, and so the traditional vampire must change also, lest the world forget. Times have changed and will continue to change, if the vampire can keep his/her ideas in the present while watching the past for inspiration, the vampire can only prosper. Technology will grow and the vampire must keep abreast of the new information, otherwise the masses will forget – and without memory and belief, what is the vampire?

Many lifestylers are keen to brand themselves in vampiric fashion, and some favour extreme body modification. One piercing, known as 'The Vampire', aims to give the appearance of a vampire bite. A metal bar is punched through the skin of the neck and finished with decorative balls – it is made more 'realistic' with the use of red decorative ends. While tattoos of vampiric or occult subjects are always popular, extreme and very primitive modification of branding and scarification (the cutting of the skin in order to create a pattern of scars) is now becoming increasingly popular. Some people wish to have personal symbols, fetish animals, or other meaningful designs or patterns cut or scarred on to their bodies. Although extreme piercings and scarifications are usually performed by qualified professionals, some people perform the cuts themselves, and make the cutting permanent by rubbing cigar ash or tattoo ink into the cutting.

Many lifestylers wear temporary fangs, while others have permanent crowns fitted or permanent implants. Some dental technicians manufacture temporary fangs that are worn over the teeth. They mould acrylic into a plate that forms a bridge under the upper front teeth.

Most popular, however, are ready-to-wear fangs, which are

bought in Gothic shops and novelty shops. There are as many different styles of fangs as there are movie vampires, and indeed many models of fangs are inspired by and named after the actor who sported them – Lee/Dracula type (canines), Nosferatu type (incisors), or even Interview with the Vampire type (doubled).

'Dracula Fangs' are the latest American imports to the UK and are the choice dentalwear for professional actors, due to the fact they are realistic, can be inserted at a moment's notice and – crucially – are easy to talk with. The innovative patented formula uses thermoplastic and boasts a unique custom partial plate 'to fit your bite perfectly'. The fangs are presented in a coffin-shaped box. These fangs were most recently sported in Wesley Snipes' blockbuster *Blade 3*. Models include 'Double Uppers', first introduced in films in 1995, which are two sets of fangs worn adjacent to each other on the upper canines, and 'Werewolf Fangs', which are both upper and lower fangs positioned over the upper and lower canines.

It is not surprising that most fangs are manufactured in America. In the US, fang-making is often considered an art form. Father Sebastian of Sabretooth Fangs, although not a dentist, is a trained dental tech and dental assistant. This means he cannot do permanent work without a licensed dentist. He makes his fangs with the highest quality dental acrylics (the same material that dentures are made from). He explains: 'The greatest pleasure for me in making fangs is getting to know someone personally and seeing the reaction and pleasure they get once they first look into the mirror. I have worked hard to build my name and have made thousands of sets of teeth in my day. Each pair I make I put my love and energy into with passion.'

Extreme care should be taken with fangs, as this sample warning indicates:

These fangs are intended for cosmetic uses only. They are sharp enough to break skin and your victim WILL need a tetanus shot if you do so. We suggest you do not bite bats, cats, dogs, people or small woodland creatures. Do not sleep with your fangs in. They might fall off and you could swallow them. If you need to clean your fangs, simply put them on and brush your teeth with regular toothpaste. DO NOT use blood capsules. They will stain your fangs pink. Please be aware that smoking will also darken your fangs.

Dental implants, by contrast, are very expensive and involve considerable pain and effort to be made perfect. The canines are removed and titanium posts are surgically implanted into the gaps. These posts then have to be left in place while the body grows bone cells around them to bed them in. Once the healing has taken place, 'false' teeth can be fitted onto the pegs and one can determine the shape of the fangs. Tooth filing is becoming ever more popular in the US and has now begun to appear in the UK. It involves filing down the enamel of the teeth to form distinct points, but is not recommended, as it weakens the teeth.

Robbie Drake is a Master Fangsmith and the only UK member of The Fangsmith Guild. He has over twenty years experience in the special-effects and make-up industry and has created hundreds of theatrical custom-made fangs for film and TV, as well as individuals. Robbie started to specialise in fangs after he made a set and got requests after wearing them himself.

Robbie offers a variety of styles, including the most popular: the original Dracula design (the 'Classic'), a single set of fangs on the canines. Other styles include the 'Lilith', fangs which sit one tooth forward from the canine, on the lateral tooth. This type, he claims, often suits women better. There are different styles reminiscent of certain films. For example, triple sets as used in *Interview with the Vampire* and short canine and long lateral, as seen in *The Lost Boys*.

The first stage in fang-fitting is the casting of the teeth and, following this, the fangs are made from dental acrylic which are moulded to a person's teeth and colour matched. As the fangs are moulded exactly to the tooth they slot into place securely and do not require adhesive.

Robbie says that it takes around half an hour to get used to talking in them and encourages practise. Whilst eating with fangs is not recommended, drinking is a possibility. With good care, the fangs can last for many years.

Not all lifestylers are solely concerned with appearance alone, however, and often their ideas extend beyond purely aesthetic concerns. Some choose to incorporate a vampiric element into important life ceremonies, like weddings. When London fangsmith Robbie married Tracey in Chislehurst Caves in Kent, the occasion had a strong vampire theme. The caves have a long history, dating from druidic times, and they are reputed to be haunted. The wedding couple arrived at the ceremony in a black carriage drawn by two black stallions with plumes. The bride wore a wedding dress of heavy black lace accompanied by a black veil and red roses – and fangs. The groom wore a black and red suit with a cane, black mask and fangs.

Another lifestyler, who models his look on the Gary Oldman portrayal of Dracula in *Bram Stoker's Dracula*, recalls marrying his bride in vampiric style:

I am Zachary Hunt. I hail from the far-flung deepest darkest corner of the south-east coast of England. Like Dracula himself, I come from the sea. Occasionally I put in personal appearances as Himself and generally scare children and old ladies. However, I always make it my mission to look good and you may often find me skulking in the shadows of old London town, scouring the vicinity for ... a fine tailor ...

I met my beautiful wife one night while we were prowling on the wing and, like bats, our radar drew us together even though we were over 200 miles apart. We were cyber vampyres and from that moment on we knew we were destined for immortal love as our spirits intertwined. On our wedding day we arrived in a blood-red coach pulled by two black horses, manes and tails flowing. We were wed at dusk by a priestess in a candle-lit deconsecrated Gothic church to the haunting music of Dead Can Dance and Lisa Gerrard. We then blessed our marriage with the planting of a sacred tree, before enjoying a feast in the Great Ruby Hall. There are few mortal pleasures I enjoy but fine wine, fine clothes and the love of my good lady are pleasure enough. I have indulged occasionally in other mortal pastimes – I particularly enjoyed reading Nick Cave's *And The Ass Saw The Angel*, and I recall with fondness Ingmar Bergman's epic film *The Seventh Seal*. Both are fascinated in their search for affirmation of their beliefs when their worlds are seemingly against them. Of course such beliefs are against my nature, but it is nature to be voyeuristic especially when a struggle is before us.

The Beautiful Deadly Children are the UK vampire scene's most decadently dressed individuals. They play Gothic festivals across the UK and their music has been described as 'Marilyn Manson crossed with Iggy Pop'. Lead singer Paul explains:

It was always our intention to live the lives of elegant vampires. And elegance is a very addictive drug. Start with the wardrobe and watch the lifestyle follow. The band and its music is just a reflection of all that. It might very well capture its essence, but it in no way dictates. I wrote a song, 'Silent Screamers', with the line 'we are from another age, we are from another time' and we are.

The Beautiful Deadly Children are like vampiric hot-house flowers. They will only thrive in the right conditions. Plant them in a seedy old pub overnight and they will surely die. Pop them into the Ritz, or the Moulin Rouge or Maxims and watch them open their little black petals. I remember going into Olivia's hotel room in Paris, one New Year's Eve, to find her tragically draped over her bed. 'I'm sick', she rasped. 'I have vomited and filled the toilet bowl with blood'. And she had. It looked like someone had run through a pig through with an electric potato peeler. Five hours later she was dancing onstage at the Moulin Rouge with enough champagne in her to kill an elephant. Attitude is all. Her sense of drama is divine.

They could never make a film about The Beautiful Deadly Children, it would need to be an opera. Rather than write individual songs, I write small collections of songs that explore a central theme.

'Silent Screamers' was inspired by silent movies, 'Hellspawn A Go Go' was inspired by the 1960s, 'Batspit' came out of a near-death experience. Others include 'Gothic Sex Machine', 'I Am A Dalek', 'Poison' and 'Every Night Is Halloween', which is our most popular song.

Everything I wear is designed by Olivia and myself. We go into sketching frenzies surrounded by incense and Rose Pouchong Tea. Olivia and I celebrate the ritual of tea-drinking in the way that most people have sex. You don't need stakes to kill these vampires, just offer them a cup of tea made with a teabag!

The Vampyre ConneXion offers a haven for lifestylers. The group meet monthly and describe themselves as 'a social group aimed at bringing together all who are interested in the vampire genre in order to have fun and make friends'. Meetings are held in a theme pub designed around the theme of Dracula, which is dimly lit and serves cocktails based on the Seven Deadly Sins. Member Becky states:

We like to visit the capital's cemeteries, our favourite being Kensal Green, where along with some great photo opportunities there are tours of the underground catacombs. Another favourite is the frequent vampire films at the cinema and we have a wonderful time baring our fangs in order to gain seats in the pub beforehand. We love dressing up to go to shows at the theatre like the Rocky Horror Show and the Dracula Ballet.

One of our annual outings is the shopping trip to

Brighton in the summer. As Brighton is an English seaside town on the south coast we don't have to worry about any exposure to the deadly rays of the sun and the day is spent wandering around the unique and cool shops en masse. Inevitably there is always one cat fight that breaks out as several people attempt to buy a wonderful piece of bat paraphernalia that they can't live without – the problem being that the shop only has one of the particular item in stock! These skirmishes are normally resolved with a pint (or several) before making our way to the pier to re-live our long-forgotten childhood with ice-cream cones and fairground rides.

The ConneXion's most outspoken lifestylers are Vampyre Master and Dark Angel. They met at a party 'many moons ago' in Kensington, 'hit it off and have been partying ever since'. They live a Gothic lifestyle but do not practise vampirism in the literal sense – they just enjoy the fantasy. Vampyre Master explains:

We are probably the most ancient of vampyres, the mother and father of all vampyres. I will let my partner Dark Angel speak for herself but as to my own dark leaning, it begins a long time ago, [I was] a mere child when I fell in love with Mina Harker on first reading *Dracula*. I was so jealous of Dracula and longed even then to have what he had – elegance, charisma, the ability to entrance and, ultimately, be utterly cruel, I have achieved all these and more.

As I grew older, and never feeling part of the world in which I lived, fantasy took over and the films of

Hammer and such like satisfied my longings. Then one day on television I saw a group in a cemetery, the Vampyre Society. At last there were others like myself who were not afraid to live and dress as we wished. I joined this society and time passed, so did the group. We then formed the Vampyre ConneXion and continued on with the fantasy. During all this time I was able to hone my skills and having always been interested and involved in the world of S&M, I gathered about me a group of willing vampyre slaves. Dark Angel and I then took over the running of the Vampyre ConneXion and we now have a very active committee and have seen the group grow in character and numbers to become the largest and friendliest vampyre group.

My own style is not just vamp or goth. I collect and wear antique or Victorian ecclesiastical garb and I have a fine collection of altar crucifixes. Our home is as pagan and Gothic as it could be, with a child's coffin in the drawing room, heavy reds and golds and in the best Victorian tradition many pieces of taxidermy, all of a predatory theme.

Blood drinking is part of the vampire legend in fiction; humans cannot exist on blood. So-called blood drinkers tend to take tiny amounts by cutting each other and it is more of a fetish. We don't know of any one personally [who drinks blood], but there are plenty of websites catering for this.

We are the 'most ancient of Vampyres' in the sense that we are in mortal years quite senior and that our interest in vampyres goes back a long way, and it's not been just a young, you'll-get-over-it type of thing.

Dark Angel shares her partner's beliefs and recently developed an interest in the real life world of bats, going as far as to adopt one, named Apple Blossom, one of the resident bats in the Cornwall Wildlife Trust's Bat Hospital. She explains:

My journey into the dark started at an early age. Being an only child until I was ten, I lived in a fantasy world fuelled by books with a leaning towards the dark, mysterious and poetic. I frightened myself reading Bram Stoker's *Dracula* when I was 12 and I used to lie awake watching my bedroom window for signs of smoke drifting in.

My mother was deeply religious and I had to attend church every Sunday, and all the festivals of the Christian calendar, and this deeply influenced an already dark soul into a love for the Gothic and ritualistic aspects of life. My early life was dominated by the Church and its rituals, incense, Gothic architecture and choirs, where we were encouraged to read the tales of saints and martyrs. This obviously became one of the major influences on my fantasies and desires as I grew up. I always felt somewhat apart from most kids of my age, who found my tastes a little bizarre.

Having learnt to read early, I soon developed a taste for myths and legends, the supernatural and dark, sensual literature. The vampyre legend has always been a particular favourite, with its promise of eternal life, and I devour any literature and film devoted to this theme with particular relish. I have been fortunate in having met Vampyre Master, with whom I have been able to share and develop my passions.

Often there is a fine line between lifestylers and real vampires – some drink blood for 'style'. But does this make them vampires or merely dedicated lifestylers who wish to add authenticity to their vampire image? Lifestylers are often deemed to be part of the 'vampire community' even though they do not crave blood or energy. Primarily this is because some lifestylers may not be aware of their true identity or perhaps have not accepted their true nature and such people may use role-playing or lifestyle as a way of coming to terms with their inner selves. In such instances, therefore, it would be incorrect to refer to certain lifestylers as 'wannabees'.

CHAPTER 9

RIP VAMPIRE SOCIETY – THE FINAL NAIL IN THE COFFIN

There used to be 15. Now there are only two. And soon there will be none. Once upon a time vampire lifestyle societies thrived. In the nineties there was Thee Vampire Guild, Whitby Dracula Society, London Vampyre Group, Erebus Rising, the Arcane, VLAD (Vampire Lovers Across Devon), Cumbrian Vampire Society and seven regional branches of the Vampyre Society. One by one they faded …

Since time began, people have felt the need to reach out to find others of their kind. In the vampire community there are many groups, clans and families that share their knowledge and support of the vampire life. Vampire lifestyle societies first formed in the UK in the eighties and reached their peak in the early nineties. These lifestyle societies differed from academic ones such as the Dracula Society and the Bram Stoker Society as discussed in Chapter 3. For lifestyle vampire societies, the vampire is commonly regarded as a supernatural being that exists in the realms of the imagination alone. It is a supernatural fantasy true to its folkloric definition – that of a reanimated corpse that has come back to life to feed off the blood of the living. In other words, the vampire does not exist for these people.

The Vampyre Society was formed in 1987 in Keighley, West Yorkshire and at its peak boasted over 500 members in the UK, Europe, America and Australia. Its aim was to unite people interested in art, literature, film and theatre dedicated to the vampire genre. There were seven areas in the UK that had branches of the society: London, South-West, Manchester, Nottingham, Wiltshire & Hampshire and Northern Ireland, with each area having its own Area Representative. President Carole Bohanan explains:

> Our society is about the appreciation of the vampire myth. Do vampires exist? Well, there probably is a part of me that would like to believe in vampires in some way. But I think I can say with 100 per cent certainty that vampires don't exist. There are people from other vampire societies who will hate me for saying that. But, if you want my opinion, I think those people need treatment.

All members received a membership card, an enamel badge with the society's logo and regular editions of *The Velvet Vampyre*, a journal of members' fiction, artwork and poetry, with reviews of recent events attended by members. Although its name conjures up images of Satanic rites carried out by moonlight and orgies of blood-letting, the Vampyre Society vehemently rejected any suggestions they were real-life vampires and denied any connections with blood-drinking cults. Perhaps the odd real vampire did slip through the net; or perhaps some just preferred to keep their blood lust secret. In general, though, the Vampyre Society were a fairly innocuous bunch and would attend theatres in vampire costumes and compare their Gothic book collections. Typically, the society restricted itself to activities such as book signings by horror film stars like Hammer Horror's 'Countess Dracula', Ingrid Pitt, and batwalks in country parks.

In the early nineties, one group of vampire fans gathered regularly every two weeks in Cathedral House, a small hotel in the heart of old Glasgow. Here, the Scottish branch of the Vampyre Society would meet in the bar of the hotel that was a few steps from the gates of the Necropolis, Glasgow's magnificent Victorian graveyard inspired by Père Lachaise cemetery in Paris. The graveyard stands on a hillside of Greek temples, obelisks and decaying mausoleums between a Gothic cathedral and the Tennent's Brewery. Vampire fans could not find a better location in the whole of Glasgow to meet.

The Glasgow society, the only branch in Scotland of the Vampyre Society, celebrated the genre by uniting people with a common interest in vampire literature, art, film and theatre.

Members ranged in ages from 16 to 60 and included a doctor, lawyer, teacher, photographer and students and would make trips to Whitby, Dracula's first landing point in Britain according to Bram Stoker's novel. Members would arrive at meetings in costume, an exotic blend of traditional 19th-century attire. One female member, who claimed to be Scotland's biggest vampire fan, said:

> I owned the first set of dental fangs in Scotland. Whereas most vampire fans have an interest in Dracula and watch the odd vampire movie, I rush out and buy everything to do with vampires. I get

excited at the mere mention of them. Most of the men I have dated are not into vampires. My last boyfriend hated my obsession and was embarrassed at having a girlfriend who wore fangs. My mum wouldn't let me read *Dracula* as a child, she thought it was unsuitable. But she let me read *Frankenstein* and *Dr Jekyll and Mr Hyde*.

Then ten years ago, when I bought the book *Interview with the Vampire* from a jumble sale, I was hooked. I now have over 500 vampire books. Basically, if it has a vampire in it, I buy it. I know people who drink blood and sleep in coffins but I would never be involved in anything like that. I was raised an Irish Catholic and the only time I would have a coffin in the house is for a wake. I also know people who have sex in graveyards, but I respect the dead.

Niki was area representative for the Glasgow branch in its heyday, from 1994 to 1996, and was a true aficionado of the myth. For her Communications and Mass Media degree, she wrote a 10,000-word dissertation entitled 'Immortal Monster: Vampire and Sociology and Culture'. Her flat was befitting for Scotland's first woman of vampires at that time. A coffin as a coffee table, a skull-shaped ashtray, a life-sized cardboard cut-out of Dracula, vampire-endorsed foam bath and Orlock, her pet rat, scurrying about, blending unobtrusively into his Draculian surroundings. She explained her fascination with vampires: 'They have the romanticism of something beautiful but damned; they have more appeal than, say, witches or werewolves, because of their beauty, immortality and, paradoxically, the loneliness, incurred by it.'

Another member stated: 'Today's youth are a sad bunch of jeans and trainers. Vampires are flamboyant. We can live a rich fantasy life through the myth.'

The society was featured on the cover of the Halloween edition of the *Big Issue* in 1996. The reporter found it difficult to believe that the two organisers of the society were vegetarians and concluded: 'Meeting a modern Scottish vampire is about as scary as having tea and scones with your granny.' Niki retaliated in the same article: 'It doesn't matter what people think about vampires, they still take the piss out of us and if they're not doing that, we're getting hassled by religious nuts who think we sacrifice children to Beelzebub.'

However, at that time publicity was mostly positive and the Vampyre Society could be relied upon to boost publicity for Dracula productions at theatres and cinemas. For the Northern Ballet Company production of *Dracula*, members turned up in their finest vampire costumes and posed for the local press. They even had boxes reserved for them. for the performance. Sometimes the Society enjoyed a charitable role, like the time they joined forces with the Blood Transfusion Unit to urge people to donate blood by posing for some humorous photos for the press.

These were essentially new times for vampire fans in the wake of films like *Bram Stoker's Dracula* and *Interview with the Vampire*. A whole new generation of vampire fans were introduced to the genre and wanted to dress up like their onscreen heroes. Naturally, the media and the general public were intrigued about these vampire fans, who embodied the romanticism and elegant costumes of these films. In common with the other branches of the Vampyre Society, the Scottish branch were aware of the need for media and elected press officers to liaise with an insatiable press. Over time, though, members learned to be cautious – on one occasion they were followed around the Necropolis by a reporter who had a tape recorder hidden in his pocket and was looking for some 'juicy' quotes.

Infamously, on 20 April 1999 two American teen Goths embarked on a murderous rampage at Columbine High School, shooting 15 other school children. The media swiftly associated the killers with the black clothes, tattoos and piercings of the Goth/vampire subculture. The Vampyre Society were fearful of a public backlash and postponed their next meeting – a first for the organisation. Despite the society's best efforts, the odd piece of negative press surfaced periodically. Once, a member named Alex, who was 23, claimed his true age was 577. Through tarot card readings he had come to believe that he had been born in Lyon, France in 1420. He had also dreamed that he had been attacked by three vampires and even claimed to have made other people into vampires. Alex lived in the east end of Glasgow and worked in a city centre burger bar; he was not allowed to wear his fangs to work, but was permitted to wear his yellow contact lenses. He claimed he was a psychic vampire and did not drink blood (he admitted he had tried drinking animal blood before but did not like the taste so vowed never to drink it again). When Alex was interviewed for a local paper and boasted about his claims, the Vampyre Society saw red and Alex was promptly expelled from it. Niki explains:

> Vampire societies and enthusiasts get bad press because of the few extremists who go around thinking they are actually vampires and drink blood. If anyone is found in the society to take part in these activities, or even support them, they are expelled.

What we do is harmless. We don't go around robbing or mugging people. Maybe if more people read like we do, the streets would be safer places.

When the meeting of the society ended as the bar closed at midnight, often a handful of members would trek across the road to the Necropolis for a late-night wander among the tombstones. Until one night, that is, when they were set upon by a group of local neds. Some of the members needed hospital treatment and the frightening incident put an end not only to the midnight strolls but signalled the demise of the society. The group moved its location to a safer city-central biker's bar/Goth drinking den and the glamour and mystique of the graveyard became a distant memory. Eventually, the Vampyre Society began to transform itself into a Goth society, with one of its latest 'recruits' confessing, 'I don't even like vampires, I know nothing about them.'

In December 1997, the national headquarters of the Vampyre Society issued a major statement. All members were informed that their president Carole Bohanan would step down as head of the society to pursue other interests, and a committee was formed to allow the society to continue. However, a few months later in April 1998, following the departure of several key committee members, the Vampyre Society was wound down and all members were reimbursed their monies. The society's bank account was closed and so too was its PO box address. Under advice from the society's solicitor, members were told that those who wished to start up a new vampire group were forbidden to use the Vampyre Society name and would have to choose a different one instead.

After the national headquarters of the Vampyre Society closed down, all affiliated branches were forced to follow suit, as only Carole Bohanan had the rights for the name to be used in that context. This signalled the beginning of the end. Despite brave promises from several groups to continue, the vampire societies never achieved the glory of their heyday and have been in decline ever since. The societies disappeared and the ones that remained transformed into Goth societies. In light of the 'vampire murders' that occurred within the next few years, some groups abandoned the now dreaded word 'vampire' – the Manchester Vampyre Society became Lost Souls and the Nottingham Vampyre Group became Nottingham Dark Souls.

One new group born out of the ashes of the Vampyre Society, and still active today, is the London Vampyre Group, which attracts individuals who are interested in film, theatre, and music in the Gothic or horror genre. Mick, 56, the most senior member of the vampire scene in the UK today, has been into Goth since 1983 and vampires since 1991. He explains how the Group came about:

There is no short answer here and an understanding of what happened has to be linked to why people would want to join a 'vampire' society in the early nineties at all. Basically, the Goth scene and its cultural spin-offs were in a decline since the mid-eighties and educated individuals on that scene wanted to be involved in something more than just going to clubs and gigs. A society which offered a network of individuals into Gothic art, literature and cinema, plus a varied attitude to music was quite welcome and many people joined in the early nineties.

I joined in mid-1991 and remained a low-profile member for some years, although living in London did mean that one was involved in what happened more than say, members in the provinces, or indeed, abroad. Part of the thrill of being in that society was all about being invited to TV and media events. Thus the Society became widely known through its media appearances, but that failed to portray a cross-section of the membership. Many outsiders would unfairly view the club as a layer of media-seeking popinjays.

I was asked to run a trip to Transylvania with a Dracula theme. I had no idea how to organise this kind of thing, but with the help of some good connections I had a 12-day tour arranged and this took 23 apprehensive travellers to Romania in the Easter of 1994. This was by all accounts a success for many reasons, but two being that it upped the profile of the society and it became something that could involve the club as a whole and not just the inner circle. This gave a number of us the confidence to organise more and more and the society also developed regional associations or branches, resulting in a significant boost to the membership.

At the head of the society was the President, Carole Bohanan, and she retained a very tight control of the club by controlling its finances. To go forward, the Society needed to have a clear set of rules and should have become an umbrella for a lot of the things which were developing at the time.

In 1994 and 1995, a group of people set up the Cumbrian Vampire Society based in Carlisle and were told by Carole Bohanan to dissolve their club and destroy their magazines since they were not official and authorised. Legal action was threatened.

It would be too far to go to describe the Vampyre Society as a cult group, it did contain a lot of cult characteristics.

In the autumn of 1995 it was our turn, as we 'disagreed with the aims of the society', six of us were told to leave the Vampyre Society.

Our immediate reaction was to get together and form up our own loose grouping with the name 'the London Vampyre Group', which we decided on in about five minutes in the Phoenix Theatre Bar. We drew up our constitution, which reflected our view of how to develop a club – at that time we would encourage more networking and versatility on the scene and to this end we chose to circulate a free information leaflet. I think some of us actually believed that we would get back into the Vampyre Society. That was not to be, but also we were not ready to set up another club as there was too much of that sort of diversity anyway – we already had Thee Vampire Guild, the Whitby Dracula Society and some other groups as well.

We progressed as a club by having decision meetings every three months, regular pub meetings and parties, and, of course, other big events like trips to Transylvania, New Orleans, Dublin and Egypt. In time we developed our magazine, *The Chronicles*, and decided to have formal membership arrangements. Most of us have relatively normal jobs and the group gives us a chance to escape and indulge our fantasies. One character, Louis, would arrive at meetings in Regency costume while another, Count Alexander, claimed he was an exiled Hungarian noble.

We have contact with sanguine vampires from time to time, but they tend to be private people who practise by agreement in their own circles, and these can be found on the internet by anyone who is serious about finding out. Blood-drinking or blood fetishism isn't really what we are about, since we see ourselves as a grouping flowing from a contemporary subculture with its origins in the decadent aesthetic. Fascination with blood or body functions is a separate sensuous pursuit which may or may not be hostile to us. Unfortunately, blood drinking can be seen as a predatory activity, and, since we act as an open organisation, we are publicly accountable – we ensure that it is not a part of our activities and cannot be portrayed as such.

We haven't barred anyone for such practices, since within the context of what we do they would be private and we would not know about them. I have seen TV programmes about the scene in America, where they are supposed to have blood-drinking clubs, but I think that says something about the USA, and the makers of those 'documentaries' had to go to the States because they could find no evidence in Britain.

One thing about 'blood drinking' is that we don't actually do it, but the society finds it perfectly acceptable for Catholics and High Church Protestants to drink blood when they take Communion. I find it hypocritical that this isn't [regarded as] equally disgusting, especially since the Church says that 'wine into blood' is not symbolic but has to be regarded as a real miracle!

Attempts were made to unite the various vampire societies throughout the UK and achieve the glory of their heyday under the Vampyre Society. In 1997, Vampire Exchange and Information Network (VEIN) was set up in order to attempt to coordinate the activities of the different vampire clubs and societies and to provide public information as to what was going on. The year was also the centenary year for Bram Stoker's *Dracula*, which was good for the scene as there was heightened interest in vampires in general and each organisation benefited from extra members.

However, in July 2001 something happened that was to lead to the demise of vampire fans in public and their retreat underground – or online worlds. After German 'vampire' murderers Manuela and Daniel Ruda killed a friend and drank his blood, the world's media turned its attention to vampire societies and their members. Even worse for members, the murderers had claimed they had learned vampirism in the UK. This only served to heighten the negative light the societies were cast in. Four months later, a 'vampire' murder hit the headlines again with the case of Matthew Hardman. And thirteen months after that, Alan Menzies murdered his friend Thomas McKendrick – on the orders of 'The Queen of the Damned', he claimed.

Three vampire murders in the space of 18 months proved to be the final nail in the coffin for any fan who wanted to celebrate their love of vampires, no matter how innocent or academic they were. Every time the newspaper screamed a headline about a 'vampire' murder, attention once again focused on vampire societies. Anxious journalists would hound vampire fans imagining, and probably hoping, that they had a hotline to vampire murderers, when this was not the case at all. Not surprisingly, many vampire fans were unwilling to comment on a crime that had nothing to do with their world of dress-up vampires. When most of these fans occasionally dressed up in a cloak or stuck on a pair of plastic fangs for a laugh, they had no idea that one day they would be 'linked', however loosely, to the vampire murders.

Now the only time the press contacted vampire societies was to ask for a comment on vampiric crimes. Vampire fans were tarnished with the same brush as their namesake vampiric killers. From being press darlings every Halloween and at the launch of any spooky Dracula productions, they gradually faded from the public eye. Now, in light of the murders, vampires and vampire fans were attracting media attention that had a distinctly negative slant. The vampire murders effectively staked the future of vampires, whether the individuals concerned were full-blown real vampires or harmless vampire fans, like lifestylers. Less media exposure meant less recruits, the lifeblood of any society. If you'll pardon the metaphor, without new blood the vampire societies started dying off.

Another factor influenced the demise of vampire fans willing to share their passion with the media. The vampire murders had proved that such crimes were no longer confined to America but could – and did – happen in the UK. Germany, Wales and Scotland – in less than a two-year period, these sickening murders had come uncomfortably close to home. Of course, it was not the first time vampire societies had been linked with certain crimes. The first significant occasion was the Columbine high-school murders, but as that crime scene was thousands of miles away, attention did not focus on UK vampire fans at the time.

Although most of the societies in existence at that time changed their name, removing the word 'vampire' from their title, the London Vampyre Group did not. Mick explains why:

> The murders were not 'vampire' murders. The individuals concerned used it as an excuse to justify their behaviour. In a civilised society the individual is responsible for what they decide to do and using their esoteric 'beliefs' to explain it is unacceptable. The Germans were just screwed up and murderous, and the bloke in Wales used to read *Bizarre Magazine* a lot – not something which came up at the time. We also fail to acknowledge that most murder in the west is carried out by God-fearing men and woman – they are rarely mentioned … The case of the Germans, who said their initiations came from vampire clubs in London, put the London Vampyre Group under some scrutiny and we did get interviewed by the press and the TV, but I don't think there were any accusations which really stuck. Plus, our research showed us that the Germans were making it up – nobody knew them, nor had met them. I think the whole episode tells us as much about young people in Germany as anything else. We are happy with who we are and have evolved a kind of understanding based on accumulated experience and wisdom. I don't think anyone has major illusions about being a vampire or what suitable behaviour as a club should be. So there is little reason there to change the name.

Who knows whether the coffin lid will open again for vampires and their most devoted fans, and one day – or night – they will rise again?

CHAPTER 10

VIRTUAL VAMPIRES – ONLINE AND EVERYWHERE

Type 'real vampire' into Google and nearly 7 million results appear. The first entries include an article on vampires through historical fiction to the modern day, and 'SphynxCATVP's Real Vampires Support Page' for 'real vampires', which is for 'those who think they might be, or know someone who might be a vampire'.

The millennial years have seen a wave of people eager to invite the undead into their lives. The internet has become a significant focus for bringing together fringe groups, such as those interested in vampirism, into virtual 'communities'. The internet is now the main tool of communication and information for vampires and explains the rapid growth of the vampire scene today. There are thousands of vampire-related websites, newsgroups and chatrooms. These range from the fairly innocuous Buffy the Vampire fan sites to the darker vampire occult sites.

This new breed of online vampires seek solace and advice

on the worldwide web, as well as using the net to gather information and find donors for their blood cravings. They find each other through message boards, chatrooms and 'personals' on websites. The online vampire community is huge and crosses continents, ages and creeds. Never before have vampires had so much freedom of information and support with which to furnish their lives.

Vampire murders, negative media, the rise of AIDS – all these factors contributed to the demise of the vampire – at least, the vampire living in harmony with his non-vampire neighbours in contemporary society. If the vampire felt like sharing his secret with the world before these issues arose, there was far less chance of that happening now.

There was only one place for vampires to go: online. As vampires have evolved through the centuries, so they have adapted and sought solace in the online world. This new breed of vampire is not limited to any geographical boundaries and can choose his or her donors from anywhere in the world, having met them in the first instance online. Where once vampires needed to meet in physical locations like special nightclubs or bars within commuting distance, now they can meet online without leaving their front door.

Nor is the vampire bound to any particular group or set of rules. Never before has so much information on vampirism been available on the internet and the thriving virtual vampire communities testify to this. Thanks to the internet, vampires can gather information, receive 'training' and find donors for their cravings through message boards and chatrooms.

One effect of the internet is that the gap between American vampires and their British counterparts is lessening and it is easy for British vampires to obtain information on vampirism from our American neighbours. There are thousands of vampire-related websites, newsgroups and chatrooms and more and more of them are based in the UK. The numerous online communities for vampires include Order of the Crimson Tongues, which has eGroups in England, Scotland, Wales and Ireland.

These virtual vampires 'breed' through the internet by meeting donors and learning about feeding techniques and apparatus. After their vampirism has evolved through their new online contacts, and they have built up a rapport, these vampires can then venture out into the real world and actually meet their donors and fellow vampires. Clearly, this helps: even vampires confess to suffering an attack of nerves before entering a room of strangers.

Secrecy is the key word in the vampire's identity. The worldwide web provides the perfect cover for reticent vampires, the perfect domain for the 21st-century vampire, especially for the vampire who craves blood. Many vampires are forced to rely on the anonymity of the internet to hide their dark secret, ever fearful of being discovered and mocked by their colleagues.

While there is a lot of support for vampire lifestylers, things are very different for real vampires. For the lifestyler there is a club scene, websites and a tolerance in society. A lifestyler might be viewed by society as a little weird, but is nevertheless dismissed as harmless. It is a different matter for the non lifestyler, who is shunned by society and seen as a danger. Such individuals cannot rent rooms in nightclubs to meet others of their kind. They cannot practise their habits in public. That is why they feed their habit in their own homes, or the homes of those closest to them. Solitary vampires who are new to the scene do not have to worry about entering a room full of strangers. Geographical boundaries do not exist and it is common for vampires to correspond with other vampires thousands of miles away. Though isolated in a small town, one can meet other vampires by way of this online connection.

Intervamp was one of the first online vampire sites. It started life as a photocopied newsletter in 1990 in the Netherlands, but as demand grew it launched online in 1996. Intervamp was especially interested in non-fictional vampires and unexplained phenomena such as haunted graves and corpses that did not decay. It included an active message page that illustrated the influence of vampires on some of the people who visited the site. Here is a selection of posts from it:

I am a vampire stuck here in Brazil. I am 444 years old.

I am a vampire 135 years of age. If there are any mortals reading this that wish to become a vampire feel free to email me. I can give you info on where to find ones like myself. But I have one rule – do not question me.

To whom it may concern: I would like info on how to become a vampire.

Although there are increasingly more UK-based vampire websites nowadays, initially most UK vampires referenced and consulted American sites. Especially popular was the Sanguinarium, a resource for real vampires, which followed The Black Veil, the voluntary standard of common sense, etiquette and ideals for the vampire community.

Another popular American site is the Vampire/Donor Alliance, an internet-based support group that gives advice to vampires all over the world. It exists to serve all those who are part of the vampire community, from Gothic 'lifestyle' vampires and non-lifestylers to energy feeders and sanguinarians. The society aims to provide a domain that vampires cannot find in the real world. Their opening statement asks: 'Do you have a close friend or lover who considers him/herself a vampire? Do you allow your loved one to cut or pierce you for blood, and feel a desire to talk about your relationship (either its loving closeness, or problems you might have) but hesitate to tell other people because they'll call you a pervert or a neurotic? There is a place to call home.'

The Alliance and other similar online associations typically exist to help vampires realise their identity and help them become vampires. In fact, rarely do these real vampire sites suggest there may indeed be no such things as vampires. Just as vampire societies and lifestylers do not associate with real vampires, likewise real vampire groups like the Alliance have little time for their fantasy-prone counterparts. They explain: 'If you want to dress up, go out to a nightclub, and do the "I'm so vampiric that I can trace myself back to Vlad Tepes/Elizabeth Bathory/Lord Byron/The Comte de St Germain", be our guest. Just please don't do it around us. We're just a bunch of people who happen to be vampires, or who happen to love vampires. We have lives, not unlives. We'd like to keep it that way.'

Vampirecityuk is a group for real Vampires in the UK and Eire to meet and discuss vampirism. It was founded in June 2002 with the purpose of 'uniting the vampires of the United Kingdom'. There are currently 90 members in the group and they freely exchange advice on topics like different methods of feeding and theories of vampirism, for example whether vampirism is a life path or a choice. Most vampires, however, see vampirism as a destiny.

Vampirecityuk allows people to share their deepest feelings. In an article entitled 'A Vampire's Awakening', one man describes his path to vampirism:

> I remember when I was about five years old, I had cut my finger and noticed I was drawn to my own blood. Many people have tasted blood before from a simple cut and thought nothing of it, but I knew the taste gave me a kind of energy which uplifted me. I found in succeeding days and weeks that I would hide in the closet from my parents and feed on my own blood energy. I only needed small amounts, so simple cuts were always enough. I knew then that I was different.
>
> As I grew older in my teenage years, my focus also started to include the emotions of others, which I found was a great energy feed, especially while around groups of people. I learned in time to substitute the psychic/empathic and emotional energy for the blood energy, which was too often unavailable. I began to look into my reading while in high school and search out the meaning behind what made me different. I watched B-rated vampire movies but did not really think myself a vampire, since all I had to go on was the film industry's own attitude of making up whatever for the most money. I looked at history and what different authors had to say about vamps like Vlad and Nosferatu. But I started to come to the fact that 'true' vampires are energy feeders but just of another sort and other abilities. I knew I needed and wanted the empathic/psychic and blood energy to 'feel' well and knew it would dominate my life. I knew now I was vampire.

Becoming an adult in the 1970s found me eagerly searching the nightclub scene for worthy female souls to accommodate my energy needs. I always knew I was heterosexual so my focus has been for the most part on the female souls around me. The next step was to be easy and my most satisfying. I quickly discovered the pranic energy with the energy of sex and once combined with the blood and emotional energy was the greatest energy feed I have ever had. Vampires are energy feeders, and in almost 50 years, maintaining this energy level is a part of my health. The vamp that can adapt to differing kinds of energy from their donors is the one who will keep that health. There is a balance with all and too much is avoided as is too little.

Order of the Crimson Tongues (OCT) is an online community for vampires and has over 100 distinct points of presence on the internet, with almost 3,000 members in total. There are eGroups in England, Scotland, Wales and Ireland. The largest group in the UK is the England group, with over 100 members. OCT has no official spokespeople. Each member of OCT speaks (or remains silent) entirely on his/her own behalf. When asked how many vampires OCT could estimate were in the UK, webmaster Bholanath answered: 'I don't think such statistics are likely to either exist or be conclusive. Between the multiple definitions of "vampire" and the secrecy/ discretion of many who have a "vampyric condition", arriving at any such agreeable number seems unlikely.'

Bholanath refused to clarify why he set up the organisation in the first place, but it indicates a disagreement of current vampire politics typical of the vampire scene, where rules and codes and group politics often cause in-house fighting. Suffice to say that Bholanath perceived OCT as a 'necessity'. He explains:

> I discovered essential communications were being thwarted by ego-trippers and found this condition intolerable. Ideally, most members of the vampire community join in a quest for personal freedom of expression. In reality, many join because they have the desire or (arguable) need to know what is being said and (rapidly) spread throughout the global vampyre community. OCT exists for only one purpose: to protect free speech within the vampyre community. Membership in OCT is not exclusive. Most members of OCT are members of other groups. The primary advantage and purpose for OCT (and specifically its forums) is that one can send quickly and easily communicate to a very large cross-section of the vampyre community. The messages are scanned by the major search engines and accessible even to non-members. Further, because of the scope of OCT's audience, messages distributed through OCT (especially if important or controversial) are likely to be passed in any necessary directions even towards people who don't normally read the forum. Anything posted to OCT is not easily ignored or repressed.
>
> I encourage everyone with an interest in protecting free speech in the vampyre community to join OCT, even if they don't receive email or regularly check the messages, because this maintains the demographic significance of the eGroup and helps to empower those members of the

community who choose to use the media. Members do, however, get some perks depending upon the particular service(s) they have joined, such as access to photo areas or file areas, the ability to advertise their website, etc. However, OCT does not offer any services that can't be found elsewhere. The sole advantage to joining OCT is showing your support and concern for free speech within the community.

The Newcastle Vampire Society has been operating since May 2000 but has only recently been advertising on the internet. The society admits it has seen a growth in membership and chose London as the ideal venue to host a big gathering, due to the abundance of trains travelling there, 'and the amount of vampires already there'. The society explains the reason for their planned gatherings:

> We are coming out of hiding eventually and we have decided to host a gathering of all – or as many as we can find – sanguinarian vampires to speak of the increasing sanguinarian activity throughout Britain and even the world and share ideas and knowledge of our history so our future may benefit.
>
> We know that our kind is widely spread throughout the country and our numbers are few, but if we gather it will strengthen our relationship and make it possible to bond with each other once again like in the old times. Up here our ways are decreasing due to the lack of vampire interest and we wish to change that as well as discuss certain issues that have recently arose. We feel that we could all benefit from a meeting of minds therefore I beckon

you to respond to our invite so we can arrange a time and place, our Darkest blessings, the NVS.

However, there is also an abundance of misinformation about the vampire that can be seen in role-play gaming sites and chats and this only serves to fuel the stereotypical view of the vampire. Vampires face a continual struggle with the one-sided negative media they face. Online vampire sites, however, provide the means to counteract these misconceptions and attempt to set the record straight. The media presents one especially persistent problem, but forums and articles posted online allow vampires to create their own media:

> We are not the blood-sucking killers that the film industry would have us all believe. We want to dispel these myths and communicate the truth about our vampirism. For too long have we had to hide ourselves from those psychotic nuts who would seek us harm because of too many vampire films made with vampire hunters and 'stakes'. We will live among all humans and coexist in the society around us, while teaching those with open minds about the truth of vampirism and taking the risk of ridicule and harm... We have a high regard for life; although we feed off of the energy of others, we do not harm others or cause pain and suffering. We have gone through this world hated and feared, and misunderstood. We desire to change this and dispel these attitudes while being able to be ourselves and not persecuted.
>
> It is important that, as vampires, we blend in well with the society we are a part of; it would be foolish

for the vampire to unnecessarily reveal the vampiric nature to open ridicule and possible harm by those who hold power, whether it is with law enforcement or with those who have the ability to harm us, be it in the media or public opinion in our schools.

The media are manipulators of current events to suit their needs for the public demand. This we must always remember, for they only know what the public has learned from so many films about us that both romanticise us and advocate our demise. We have to deal with the misinformation from not only what the film industry portrays, but the bias of [the media and] other professionals who view us as killers, much like those who would do the violence that has been so recently done in schools. The reality of nuts and people with a mental aberration remind us that we are easily paired with them just because we may be wearing black or some other article of clothing.

Virtual vampires are using the technology of the internet to join forces as never before. One vampire community explains:

The Vampire Community is in need of leadership for the purposes of unity among us and survival of our kind. One of the primary goals of Lucifer's Den is this unity and survival. Many groups and organisations of the vampire community come and then disappear, However, we must not suffer this prophetic demise. We must be organised in our ability to take a place of leadership in the vampiric world and in directing a future for the vampire community. Unity of cause and dedication of purpose is the key to our survival. We cannot allow the failures of other organisations to deter us. As some have come and quickly gone, we must choose to associate ourselves carefully with each other and others on- and off-line. Leaders must be genuinely concerned about what is happening in the vampire community instead of just being the head of some group. The Vampire Community will always be here. We must make the decision to support our fellow kin in our group or we will be doomed to failure in leaving those who need our help and leadership separate and apart.

So what do vampire societies that were formed before the internet revolution feel about the rise of their virtual neighbours? Mick of the London Vampyre Group:

On the one hand, the internet has enabled easier communication between groups and individuals, and established greater opportunities for cheap and widespread publishing of one's views and ideas, so things are more open and global now. On the other, patterns of behaviour have changed in such a way that people actually do less in terms of participating and real involvement, plus surfers on the internet expect so much in return for nothing now, and insist on being both remote and anonymous.

A lot of the internet is used for indulgent self-promotion rather than actual education or enlightenment so one has to be really selective. The emergence of newsgroups and forums is a good thing, but I did notice that America went quiet after the attack on the Twin Towers and hasn't really come back even now, leading to a more European bias.

Overall, the internet is a good thing. I remember the days when the only way to do a quick communication was to write letters or make telephone calls, which took days if you were trying to contact, say, a hundred people. Now you can just send out an email and the receiver's enthusiasm can be gauged by how quick the response is. I think there is an onus on people to have contact with the internet, but, in a way, I think an organisation is entitled to expect people to take the trouble to sort that out for themselves. I still know people who don't have a telephone on principle, and, in one case, a woman who replicates her own Victorian world by not even having running water.

A final thought to conclude this chapter on virtual vampires: as the power of the internet grows, does the spread of the vampire grow with it? One real vampire site declares: 'We are becoming more organised. We have become more open in such forums as computer websites and in our neighbourhoods. This is our risk, but we will see it through for we want others to know about the true vampire.'
Some closing advice from agony aunt Katharina Katt on internet protocol for vampires:

The internet has opened a world where the vampire can feel protected, free, and truly anonymous. They know that their private identity is, in most cases, protected and they can share their true feelings, problems, and search for the truth of what they really are. Many vampires do not know what they are until they come across an internet site that has the definitions of what human living vampires really are. They find out that they are not alone. They are not abnormal freaks, or mental cases. This is quite reassuring and a breath of fresh air. With this realisation they search out others like themselves to make internet friends and sometimes even to find friends in their area so that they can meet.

Several obstacles stand in their way, however. In order to find other vampires like themselves they have to wade through a large, and ever growing, group of vampire role-players who insist they are just as real. They also have to learn how to avoid the vampires with 'god complexes' and 'immortality complexes' who insist they are superior to them and they must obey them in order to learn how to survive as a vampire. What each vampire must do is find their own truth – what is true to them. When the pieces all seem to fit, then they have found what they are looking for. What is true for me, may not be what is true for you. Therefore everyone must find their own truth. Internet sites that I recommend to avoid include what are often called 'Vampire Churches' and some 'Vampire Covens'. Some of these enforce strict rules involving reading their 'black bible' and embracing their religious views as your own. This has become quite dangerous as they also inform uninformed vampires as to what their condition is, twisting it into something it is not. There is at least one 'Vampire Church' which teaches Satanism. I would like to point out that being a vampire is more of a condition and has nothing to do with religion.

If an internet site's rules and community is based on safety, friendship, getting along with each other, and often has people that you can go to for advice but is in no way 'ruling over you' then you have found a good site and community.

Role-playing is, of course, quite different from reality, and yet it is done, in most cases, just for fun. Individuals are able to dress up in scary costumes like Halloween or stick to the more classic looks of suits and jackets and explore their new-found characters. In these worlds of imagination the sky is the limit. Anything is possible. In their role-playing world they can kill, or not kill, they can fly, be buried for centuries, and mesmerise anyone they want to bite with just a look from their eyes. Role-playing, no matter what the subject or creature it is based on, is always fun to those involved. It is a escape for reality into something new, exciting and fun. However these have very little to do with what we term as real vampires, but are based more on the mythical and fictional vampire types. The power of the internet and its own growth does not necessarily increase the growth of the vampire, however it does allow more vampires who do not know what they are to find the clues, and the pieces that will fit into their unsolved mysterious condition. Many vampires, who did not know what they were before, and perhaps never would have considered the possibility in a 'there's no such thing as ghosts' world, can today count themselves among the numbers of vampires who now know.

CHAPTER 11

UNDER A SCARLET MOON – A VAMPIRE SOCIETY UNCOVERED

'If you really can't resist the need for blood, and you have no donors, drink your own blood, it'll take the edge off. You can also try eating black pudding or drinking animal blood from a butcher/supermarket meat. This is a last resort only.'

This advice is written by a real vampire for other real vampires. It is from the Scarlet Moon Organisation, the first organisation catering for real vampires in the UK. There are no other organisations representing real vampires in this country, and most real vampire societies – online and off-line – are based in America. Real vampire groups that actively promote the drinking of blood are very rare in the UK, even rarer when they form an actual organisation. So the significance of Scarlet Moon cannot be underestimated, especially as it existed mostly unknown to the rest of the population, including the vampire community.

Scarlet Moon started up in July 1999 and was still active in 2002, though it is currently off-line. However, one can assume that members of the organisation are still active in the UK and continue to meet each other. A woman known as H. was the webmistress and founder and started the site to fill a gap in the UK vampire community, who were at that time without a central support network, either off-line or online.

H. explains:

> Since I became aware of my vampirism when I was 13 I had looked for other vampires. In the following ten years I had found nothing, even after attending the various vampire societies that existed in this country. The nearest I ever got was one night, while working in a fast food shop, and I felt a presence walk past. Unfortunately I was working in the back and couldn't see who it was. Ten long years all by myself. Then, in early '99, I got access to the Internet and discovered the vampiric community. In the following weeks I read all the sites I could find and eventually realised that there was nothing at all for vampires in the UK. A couple of weeks later I decided that I would do something myself and so I sat down at a friend's computer, and began writing the first page of the Scarlet Moon's website.

Scarlet Moon is primarily a resource for sanguine vampires resident in the UK. It provides information on vampirism, with articles offering help on problems that afflict vampires. Communication with other vampires is a vital factor in the organisation and members are encouraged to find others in their area, or anywhere in the UK, by using the members' database, posting an ad in the classifieds or by leaving a message on the message board. Scarlet Moon existed at its peak both in cyberspace and in the real world, with meet-ups in pubs and clubs. Its mission is to 'to help vampires in the UK find each other, make friends, offer advice and services to anyone who wants it'. Other services that the Scarlet Moon offers include an ordering service for sanguine vampires so they can buy medical supplies for blood-drinking.

Scarlet Moon offers advice on many aspects of vampirism, and is essential reading on health issues, the site's 'vampire personal ads' provides a great way to meet other vampires and exchange information. Safety is always a paramount issue for all serious vampire practices involving blood:

> Visitors to the site deep down in yourself you know whether this is for real or if you are just kidding yourself. There are no tests that can be done to prove if you really arc a vampire but there are indicators. A better sense of hearing, night vision and smell. Sudden attacks of the Hunger with a great desire for blood. Ability to finish people's sentences and pre-guess what they are going to do next (empathic abilities). Better resistance to disease, stronger than the norm. There are other smaller details, but these are general indicators.

Scarlet Moon strives to differ from other vampire organisations and boasts a no-nonsense approach:

> We have no religious bent, no hierarchy, no role-playing-based fake history, no bullshit. What you see is what you get. What we want is the truth, the online vampiric community is confusing to new vampires and Joe Public enough as it is and we don't want to add to it with more mystic mumbo-jumbo.

The social aspect is important and Scarlet Moon strives to solve the issues of isolation that many vampires face as they hide their secret from their families and society. The site includes 'vampire events listings' to counterbalance the fact that there are no events catering for real vampires in the UK. Parties are held regularly, with at least one Scarlet Moon party every year. As membership grew, so did plans for informal regional get-togethers in pubs, with London being the main focus, due to the relatively high number of vampires living there, including several that H. knows personally.

Certainly the organisation has grand plans, though it remains to be seen whether these will reach fruition. H. intended to buy property cheaply at auction, convert it and let it out exclusively to real vampires. Income from the property would then be used to fund the Scarlet Moon in addition to buying more property for the same purpose. Perhaps in the not too distant future there will be secret vampire villages throughout the UK. This desire to physically unite vampires distinguishes Scarlet Moon, as up till then vampires were scattered around the country in isolation. At last here was a person willing to unite people – and even become their landlady.

With the anonymity afforded by the internet, sanguine vampires can post messages to find others of their kind on the Scarlet Moon noticeboard. One Scottish male blood drinker known as Venik described himself as: 'Normal type of guy, not particularly Gothic or anything. Smiles a lot.' Another known as Grand Angel Sexay posted the following message:

> Wonderfully eccentric or strange individual who has made his lust for blood no secret. Can usually be seen in dull colours, loves black clothes especially his PVC jeans! Short bleached hair. Dislikes people

who bullshit about being a vampire, and only likes real, true vampires, no fakes. Has a love for life, blood, and WWF. I've always been called Angel, before Buffy, so no connection between us. I go by name Angel de Luca, and almost never use my real name. I like to confuse, induce fear, but also to be friendly. I also for some reason have a mask I wear to scare the hell out of people. It goes well with my cloak and is great for parties.

Since Scarlet Moon's main purpose is to help real vampires in the UK find other vampires within the UK, there is a members' database and a message board.

In her article 'For Those Who Wish To Become Vampires', H. states:

I knew there would eventually come a moment when someone would ask me if they could be 'turned'. So here comes the ultimate statement to those who come here wishing to be made into a vampire. SORRY, BUT I CAN'T. I CANNOT BITE YOU AND TURN YOU INTO A VAMPIRE. The reason? We are all born this way. We are not undead. We are alive. Most of us have either gone through what I call vampire puberty or have been 'awakened' to our nature but all of us have been vampires since the moment we were conceived. I'm sorry to disappoint you and I sympathise, the modern myth of the vampire is seductive. The sheer power, never having to fear another human being, never having to fear growing old and feeble, having forever to do all the things you've ever wanted, who wouldn't want a chance at that. But the reality is very different. We grow old slower than normal humans but we do grow old and eventually die. We do have abilities that most people don't but we cannot shape-shift nor do we possess supernatural strength. And we are always hungry. At our most basic level we are all natural predators, whether we like it or not and asking to be 'turned' by people you don't know puts yourself in danger. The majority of us are reasonably nice people but there are vampires who will prey on those gullible enough to believe in them. I don't wish to sound patronising but you run the risk of coming to serious harm when dealing with real vampires. Even we can come to harm when dealing with our own kind.

One essay on the site was entitled 'Coming Out of The Coffin, or How to Tell Someone You're a Vampire'. It explained how a male site member, C., who is not a vampire, discovered by accident the website of his friend, the webmistress H. of Scarlet Moon. He explains:

When I actually found her website and saw what it was about, I think that the only word that can describe what I felt was 'gobsmacked'. Here was a perfectly normal woman and suddenly I have not only to accept the existence of 'real' vampires, but also have to accept that she is one. I think that I tried to tell myself that the whole website was part of some glorified role-playing game, but it was too obviously genuine. I left her website and for a while considered just pretending that I had never found it.

As H. had kept the site a secret from all her 'non-vampire' friends, including C. she was angry it had been discovered and also fearful of her friend's reaction. Thankfully, they remained friends and C. even had his blood tested to make sure it was free of HIV and hepatitis so that he could consider being a blood donor for H. He explained how he came to accept her vampirism:

> She pointed me to the link to Sanguinarius's page for more information. By the end of a telephone call I felt we had both been reassured. I have never had any problem with the blood-drinking aspect of this type of vampirism.

Indeed, telling someone that you are a vampire is a difficult prospect and often the best thing is to rely on one's instincts in deciding to reveal one's vampirism. H. advises testing people's reactions by asking them about the existence of real vampires. Depending on this reaction, and whether they are open to the subject, then one can proceed to share vampire secrets. Sometimes things can be unpredictable – H. goes on to recount her own example, where her friend C. discovered her site by chance. Fearful of his reaction, she was relieved that he believed she was a vampire. The lesson is that one can never predict the reaction – in some cases, H. warns, friends may even ask for proof.

As a result of the site being discovered, advice was posted on the Scarlet Moon site to avoid detection on the web by other non-vampires. This included using different online aliases and setting up a separate email account with a fake identity. This separate identity should be used only for vampire-related correspondence. Vampires are advised to avoid hosting a website as it is likely that real details would have to be given when signing up. As email can always be traced to an organisation or a building, the ideal scenario would be for the vampire to go to a cyber-café every time they posted a message.

Another member also shared his experiences of 'coming out' to a friend of his. Drunk after a night out, he felt confident enough to send a text message on his mobile phone to his friend. He revealed to her he was a sanguine vampire but far from the friend being surprised and asking him to explain this term, she understood. Naturally the friend wondered whether he had only confessed to her in order for her to become a donor. He assured her that it was not the reason at all – he had simply wanted to open up to someone.

Members of Scarlet Moon can access articles on vampire issues, specifically advise on problems that vampires face. In a section entitled 'Common Questions of the Newly Awakened', H. was asked questions such as 'Can I trust my parents?' Not surprisingly, the answer to this is a resounding 'no':

> Parents don't react well to finding out that their darling child has taken to drinking blood. Some refuse to have anything further to do with their vampire child, but many will think that you need to see a psychiatrist or, even worse, have you committed to a mental hospital. I don't know anyone who has been honest with their parents and not regretted having done so. I haven't told my parents and have no intentions to do so.

Other questions included: 'How do I know who to tell about this?' One member replied:

Personally I prefer not to tell my friends that I'm a vampire, but they often accuse me of being a vampire jokingly because of my nocturnal habits. It can be hard sometimes having to deny my nature to them but I don't trust telling them because of their attitudes to the subject in general. Testing people's reactions to the existence of real vampires before actually telling them is often a good idea.

An article available on the site entitled 'Energy Feeding' suggests methods the psychic vampire can use to obtain energy when they find themselves without a donor. The vampire is advised to feed from a group by going to a shopping centre and trying to draw energy from the passing crowds. A nightclub is recommended as a good feeding ground, as there is usually a lot of people giving off excess energy that the vampire can draw in: 'With feeding from gigs you have to remember that the people's emotions are being manipulated by the performer, so if you do not like feeding from dark emotions then perhaps a Portishead gig is not the best place to feed.'

Aside from social activities that makes them similar to lifestyle and academic vampire societies, there is one thing Scarlet Moon provides that is generally taboo with all UK vampire societies. The site contains explicit information on blood-drinking and provides an ordering service via which vampires can get supplies such as knives. There is even a page on feeding techniques. In a section entitled 'Feeding Techniques for Vampires' there are diagrams on the safe use of various instruments, how to obtain them and the best areas of the body on which to use them.

According to Scarlet Moon, most vampires use scalpels for cutting chiefly because they are easily available, cheap and very sharp. Another benefit of scalpels is that the wounds caused by them close up quickly due to the fact that the cut is clean and thin. Moreover, scalpels cause very little tissue damage and less scarring than razor blades or knifes. Disposable scalpels are ideal, as they come in a sterile vacuum packet and these can be bought from art and craft shops and DIY stores. Keeping blades sterile is recommended – this can be done by heating the blade over a flame or by using antibacterial pads from a pharmacy. Vodka with a high alcohol content can also be used also to sterilise blades and all sterilisation should be done immediately before cutting. As the site states: 'With common sense scalpels are fairly safe to use, just remember not to cut too deeply, never slice into veins or arteries and never ever cut on a donor's neck (even if they ask you to).'

A self-confessed 'greedy' vampire, H. personally does not like lancets as they produce very small amounts of blood. But she recommends them for vampires with squeamish donors worried about losing too much blood, especially 'Autolet lite', which is 'easy to use and comes with three different platforms which allows the penetration depth to be adjusted'. Another advantage with lancets, she points out, is that lancet wounds can easily be passed off as insect bites.

Syringes are used by many vampires but are not recommended by Scarlet Moon unless the vampire is trained in safe blood-drawing. A relative of H. is a trained phlebotomist and recounts a story of a needle that was not inserted properly and caused the patient's hand to swell to double its normal size due to a swelling of clotted blood within the tissues. Syringes do have advantages, as the site explains: 'Syringes are wonderful little things, you can extract larger amounts of blood while leaving virtually no visible mark.' If the vampire does not have access to a medically trained person, or is unable to take a course on this subject, Scarlet Moon advises studying a book on phlebotomy and its techniques. The site asserts that 'in an ideal world all donors would be trained phlebotomists'.

Biting is not endorsed by Scarlet Moon, as there is often a risk of infection from bacteria in the mouth. But if a vampire is adamant about biting, H. recommends gargling with an antibacterial mouthwash first.

With feeding techniques examined, the next step is supplies and precisely where to buy lancets, syringes and sharps bins for disposal of used syringes and scalpels. The site provides the phone number for a mail-order service for diabetics. Naturally, vampires should not admit why they were really buying the supplies and H. advises telling the salesperson they are mild diabetics who use insulin. A catalogue would then be sent free to them.

Scarlet Moon also provides advice on aftercare of wounds inflicted during feeding, how to avoid infection and scarring, and also general care to avoid diseases. Aftercare of wounds is vital and medical swabs, or Dettol on cotton pads, should be used for cleaning wounds. Tea Tree cream or Aloe vera gel is effective for reducing scarring and should be rubbed on the wound daily to aid healing. Neither does the site shirk from advising on the worst-case scenario of aftercare: 'If, in the process of feeding, you do have an accident and perhaps nick an artery, do not hesitate to call 999 and ask for an ambulance. Knowledge of basic first aid is also a good idea but if you have none and you get a gusher then take this action.' The site then proceeds to offer advice on stemming the blood flow – the bleeding donor should tie an item of clothing such as a T-shirt tightly around the wound and pressure should be applied to slow the flow. This should be maintained until help arrives.

Scarlet Moon are aware of the main risks faced by sanguine vampires – diseases such as HIV, syphilis and hepatitis A, B and C. Hence, the site recommends blood tests from new donors before feeding from them and that all donors should have regular tests. In addition, vampires are advised to be wary of donors who may have travelled to tropical countries, as malaria and sleeping sickness are all blood-borne parasites.

Although some vampires drink fresh animal blood, Scarlet Moon does not recommend this practice. The main disadvantage of animal blood according to H. is the risk of catching diseases transmittable from animals to humans and parasites from fresh animal blood. Although H. claims to know vampires who enjoy animal blood.

The site allows members to share advice on feeding. Topics include 'taking the edge off', 'cravings and withdrawals' and 'circular feeding'. Members can discuss alternatives for times when they cannot obtain blood: 'If the hunger gets really bad I drink tomato juice and try and convince myself that it is blood or I eat black pudding. If I can't get at these I try to lose myself in music but these are never as fulfilling as blood. I try to avoid drinking my own blood. I don't want to make it a habit 'cos I think that could go bad easily.'

The site attracts vampires who have nowhere else to turn for information. One vampire states:

> I'm 17 and for a long time I have been fascinated with vampires. I have a passion and a deep fascination for blood. Many have said I need to seek medical help and for a while I thought they were right but as I was scanning the web I found out there are a lot of people who seem to be the same. Now I

strongly believe that I am a vampire. I would like to know more about this way of life and advice on how to go about this life from someone wiser and who has been through this. Any help is appreciated. PS: I will only tolerate seriousness in this matter.

Scarlet Moon, like most real vampire associations, exists almost exclusively to help vampires realise their identity and help them become vampires. In fact, rarely do these real vampire sites suggest there may indeed be no such things as vampires. H. advises those with vampire tendencies:

You have to accept what you are, it cannot be changed and denying it will only bring you heartache and grief. As you come to terms with what you are, take the time to make friends with other vampires, either through message boards or personals. Don't be afraid to ask questions, real friends will be happy to help no matter how stupid you think the question is. Explore the online community, there is a lot of information out there.

Scarlet Moon provides a rare opportunity for vampires to converse without judgement and offers a safe haven for vampires to confide their deepest feelings. One member said of her vampirism:

It's not something that you can bottle up and hide when it is such a big part of your life. It affects your moods, eating habits and sexuality. The big problem, however, is that it is not something you can be open about. I am only open about it with a select few of my non-vampiric friends, and only because I knew that they would be cool with it. The better you understand vampirism, the better you can deal with it. Some people try to ignore it, and it can destroy them. Control your beast, don't let it control you.

The group is extremely careful about their existence being secret to non-vampires, and it seems likely that concerns about the group being discovered forced the organisation off-line entirely. When by chance members realised that Scarlet Moon was linked to search engines, shock waves resulted, as H. had deliberately avoided submitting the site to any search engines, anonymity being a key factor of the group.

So secret is Scarlet Moon that even the most dedicated vampire fan was unaware the group or its website existed. If an organisation like this can be formed and expand a network of vampires, all the while managing to escape the attention of society in general, it's a fair assumption that there are many more such groups operating in the UK today.

CHAPTER 12

I BELIEVE IN VAMPIRES – GODS, BIBLES AND SATAN

I am a Vampire.

I worship my ego and I worship my life, for I am the only God that is.

I am proud that I am a predatory animal and I honor my animal instincts.

I exalt my rational mind and hold no belief that is in defiance of reason.

I recognize the difference between the worlds of truth and fantasy.

I acknowledge the fact that survival is the highest law.

I acknowledge the Powers of Darkness to be hidden natural laws through which I work my magic.

I know that my beliefs in Ritual are fantasy but the magic is real, and I respect and acknowledge the results of my magic.

I realize there is no heaven as there is no hell, and I view death as the destroyer of life.

Therefore I will make the most of life here and now.

I am a Vampire.
Bow down before me.
(© The Vampire Temple)

This is 'The Vampire Creed'. It belongs to the Vampire Temple, an international church devoted to the vampire religion and which claims to be the only true vampire religion in the world. At present no similar organisation operates in the UK, but the US-based organisation claims geographical boundaries are unimportant and thanks to internet teaching, membership meetings take place throughout the world. 'We are everywhere,' the Vampire Temple asserts.

For many, such as the members of the Vampire Temple, vampirism is more than a lifestyle or a philosophy. It is a religion. Lucas, the administrator of the Temple explains:

> The Temple of the Vampire is the only authentic Vampire religion in the world, directly sponsored by and directed by the advanced Vampires which the Temple refers to as the Undead Gods. The Temple has been registered with the US government since 1989 and the Temple Priesthood has been registered since 1988 as the Temple of the Dragon. We have an international membership, worldwide in-person meetings, a dedicated Priesthood and an extensive body of published literature apart from an in-depth, multi-layered internet message board and website.
>
> Real Vampires don't drink blood. That is a myth that has been perpetuated to hide the truth from the mundane masses. We take the excess Lifeforce radiated from human beings and, in turn, give this Lifeforce to the more advanced Members of our

Family, who then, also in turn, return this Energy for Vampiric Metamorphosis. This completed 'circuit' of Energy exchange is known as Communion and is the fundamental process required for the practice of true Vampirism.

Vampirism is a religion which meets all the common social criteria of a religion: the Temple practises the ceremony of Communion; seeks out those who are of the Family but were unaware of their Heritage; practises an ethical code of behaviour known as Temple Law; possesses a creed, clergy, organisational structure; and celebrates the season holidays of the equinoxes and solstices. A summary of the fundamentals of the Vampire religion is found in The Vampire Creed. The Temple of the Vampire does not recognise 'vampire lifestyles' and absolutely forbids blood drinking or criminal activity for our members.

Members are asked to obey four rules. Firstly, members must be law-abiding and not commit crimes that would cause them to be incarcerated. Secondly, members must not drink physical blood, as this would expose the Temple to criminal liability. Thirdly, members must not represent the Temple without written permission, although they are allowed to reveal the public website address to non-members. Members are not allowed to join any organisation that attacks the Temple's image or supports criminal activity or blood-drinking. Membership of racist or neo-Nazi groups is also contradictory to the teachings of the Temple. 'Neither does the Vampire Temple welcome any other member supporting any organization or cause that claims to be vampire. The

Temple recognises no other authority than its own as the true Vampire Family.' Any members who break these rules are immediately excommunicated.

The Temple has an active priesthood and its own bible. To join the Temple one must order the Vampire Bible, which also bestows lifetime membership to the Temple. The Vampire Bible contains information on the practice of authentic vampirism through contact with the 'Undead Gods' and the 'Advanced Vampires', who are the founders and mentors of the Vampire Temple. Chapters in the Vampire Bible include 'The Secret Methods of Vampirism' and 'The Coming Apocalypse'.

A common misconception is the belief that all vampires worship the Devil. Does vampirism as a religion for the Temple identify with a God or Satan figure? Lucas explains:

> The Vampiric religion defines the individual as his or her own god. As part of priesthood training, the traditional (and specious) theological arguments for an anthropomorphic god are presented and demonstrated to be irrational. The cultural elements that characterise a god are revealed to be identical to the higher state of consciousness that becomes the norm for the Vampire. Additionally the Vampire is dedicated to the mastery of life on Earth. The acquisition of wealth, health, life extension and physical immortality are all critical issues for the Vampiric god who is the individual Vampire. The Judeo-Islamic-Christian god figures are recognized as mythological characters that serve specific psychological needs for ordinary human beings. The Temple is not opposed to human religions. The Vampire religion maintains the tradition that the

current modern mass religions were started (and are often still guided) by Family members for very practical purposes. In fact the Vampire Family endorses the value of human religions as they serve the purpose of offering meaning to the lives of mortals and inculcating a subservient attitude toward the gods.

Does the Vampire Temple believe that more people in current times are turning to vampirism as a religion? Lucas:

We know this for a fact. The Temple was given permission to come into public existence in 1989 in order to attract and educate those with the Vampiric Potential in a conscious manner. The growth of the Temple since that time has been steady and demonstrates that the experiment is proving to be a success. The Temple offers an approach to life that rejects faith or belief but, instead, is entirely based upon the motto 'Test Everything. Believe Nothing'. Those who have the Vampiric Potential are attracted to this straightforward and refreshingly sane concept. We have always been here. Now, for the first time, the Teachings of the Vampire religion have been given permission for limited public dissemination. The results have been dramatic and satisfying. We are not for everyone. We are elitist and for many good reasons. We are only for those who have the Vampiric Potential and the willingness to actualise it. The rewards are many for those who discover who and what they truly are and always have been. Further, we truly do not care what non-members or groups do at all as long as they simply

leave us alone. It may be difficult for many to
understand that we take our religion seriously but
we do.

The Temple is a secret society – correspondence from The
Temple includes a discrete symbol to denote the sender. The
Temple do not seek media and have survived for over 17 years
by discretion and selective procedures of who gains admittance
to their doctrine. The Temple explains: 'Vampirism is not
easily understood and is reserved only to those who are born to
the Blood, those who feel the draw of the Night, those who find
that they are different from the herd of humanity and glory in
that difference. The Temple is not for everyone. Many are
Called. Few are Chosen. Fewer still Enter.'

The Vampire Temple disassociates itself from other
vampire groups, especially various lifestyle groups and
individuals who proclaim to be 'real' vampires, and in
particular sanguine vampires. The Temple has its own beliefs
and often these are incompatible with such groups, many of
which tolerate blood drinking, which is expressly forbidden by
The Vampire Temple. The organisation maintains that only
they hold the key to true vampirism: 'Mortal life is swift and
short. You have this one chance to reach out to Us and
become a true member of the Religion of the Rulers, a
Vampire, an immortal Master of the earth, or be lost to the
winds of time.'

Such is the level of false reports about the Vampire Temple
that there is a 'Public Rumour Clearinghouse'. Two recent
rumours expelled are detailed here:

Does the Temple teach that you must die to join
the Undead?

No. Quite the contrary. The human religions are those that teach that one must die to 'go to heaven' and join with 'God'. We don't. The Temple has always Taught that the Undead are Themselves embodied as covered already here and rather clearly (I should think) in The Vampire Creed. The trick to understanding what the Temple is actually Teaching is to read what is in plain public view. Don't rely on what others say. Read what We say.

Does the Temple teach that Vampires are an alien race?

No. The Temple Teaches that the cutting edge of humanity has the Potential to evolve into a higher form that has traditionally been called the Vampire or the Gods. Where and how the human race evolved may be interesting in and of itself but still has nothing to do with the primary intent of the Temple: personal survival. I suspect this rumour came from someone watching too many re-runs of *The X Files*.

Although for most people vampirism is not usually governed by any specific religion, and religion is not necessary for vampirism, it can exist alongside it. Nonetheless, vampirism is practised by many as a religion. Unlike The Vampire Temple, who forbid blood drinking, other blood drinkers liken this to a deep religious experience. For many, vampirism dictates their beliefs and hence vampirism is often viewed as a cult rather than a state of being. The union of religion and vampires is not a new one. In folklore, the vampire was often deemed to exist outside the realm of God – non-baptised individuals, heretics and the excommunicated were commonly viewed as vampires in past times.

The misconception that all vampires worship the Devil still persists. When one vampire was asked, 'I'm a vampire, do I have to worship the Devil?' he responded: 'No. There is absolutely no ideological, religious or philosophical requirement or implication in being a living vampire. If you are a living vampire, human or non-human, I feel entirely confident that you are not possessed by a demon, a minion of Satan or condemned to Hell.'

Still, for many, vampirism is related to the occult and some vampire religions have their origins in Satanism although Satanism is not always exclusively practised by many vampires. One vampire explains: 'You do not need to abandon God or change your religious beliefs. I personally know living vampires who are devout Christians, Pagans, Wiccans, Taoists, Satanists and atheists. I happen to be a Pagan with a Masters of Divinity degree who preaches regularly in Unitarian-Universalist churches, myself.'

In her book *Vampires Among Us*, Rosemary Ellen Guiley meets Londoner Damien, and her German boyfriend, Damon. They are featured in the chapter 'Dancing with Satan'. Guiley notes that their Satanic affiliation is unusual as most vampires vigorously disassociate themselves from all things Satanic. Damien said she believes vampires are the children of Satan. 'God was supposed to create the Earth. Satan created all the vampires. I really do believe that.'

Vampire Master and Dark Angel of the Vampyre ConneXion explain their views on the occult and its connection with vampirism: 'We don't think there is a link between vampirism and the occult. Some people might think it is associated with the Devil, but we have to remember that vampires are all a fantasy.'

Mick from the London Vampyre Group concurs when asked if there any connections between vampirism and Satanism:

> I am going to start off by saying NO. A proper answer would require you to define 'vampirism' and 'Satanism', since both these terms can mean conflicting things. If your question is 'do members of vampire clubs tend to also be involved in worship of the devil' then it is a definite no. I find it hard to see 'vampirism' as a proper term since we know that vampires don't exist – it's in our Frequently Asked Questions. If you mean blood drinking, that isn't really anything to do with vampires as they are fictitious and fantastic. Saying anything else is not about understanding a phenomenon, but rather a description to be used in a role-play situation. Satanism isn't necessary devil worship as the Church of Satan really sees itself as an inverse of the Christian church and not just a rival, meaning that worship and belief are different if not non-existent. This question is posed mainly by fundamentalist Christians or the tabloid press trying to make a point, and being an atheist myself and becoming more hostile to religion and irrational belief by the day, I think it is always loaded with the worst assumptions. Looking at it from where I stand, the Christian church in our culture has caused more damage than devil worshippers ever could – the burning of at least 100,000 women for witchcraft? Have they ever excused it?

While the vampire may not be in league with Satan, the vampire is often viewed as an anti-God figure. One only has to consider the common belief of the crucifix to ward off vampires. Indeed, perhaps Stoker chose his anti-hero as a religious symbol. Stoker's Dracula was deemed to symbolise many things, from immoral impulses suppressed by society to a stand-in for Christ. Gordon Melton, author of *The Vampire Encyclopedia*, ponders this issue further. He states: 'Most modern novelists and screenwriters have agreed that vampires usually were created by the bite of another vampire. However, this left them with a question "Where did the first vampire come from?" Satanism emerged as the primary answer.'

Gavin Baddeley is considered one of the world's leading experts on Satanism. In 1995 he was invited to join the official Church of Satan by the late Anton LaVey, who led the movement for over 30 years. Baddeley's published books include *Lucifer Rising, Goth Chic: A Connoisseur's Guide to Dark Culture* and *Dissecting Marilyn Manson*. In the chapter 'Dark Angels of Sin' in *Goth Chic*, Gavin Baddeley states:

> There are many similarities between what motivates some to declare themselves Satanists and others to claim to be vampires: both are Gothic roles that set the adherent apart from the mundane world, deliberately alienating them from mainstream society. Both roles are implicitly misanthropic. The membership of a Satanic order is akin to symbolically turning in your membership card of the human race, becoming as close to most people's idea of a monster as possible without crossing the boundary into sociopathic behaviour. Those who claim to be afflicted by the curse of the vampire are

making a similar gesture, but the role requires the sociopathic activity of blood drinking. However, aspirational vampires effectively defang themselves by identifying with a mythical creature risen from the grave, implicitly attacking their own credibility. You can literally become a Satanist in a way that you cannot be a vampire. Perversely, many would-be vampires go even further in compromising their lifestyle, disavowing blood drinking altogether – adopting a controversial role only to try to redeem it by portraying themselves as misunderstood, saddled with the condition against their will.

The Ordo Anno Mundi (OAM) is a magical society that offers full training in traditional witchcraft, including werewolf and vampire transformation. It has members in all areas of the UK, and many overseas. The organisation was founded on 18 March 1985 in Staffordshire, but in 2002 its headquarters transferred to a Singapore box number. As of November 2003 there were over 400 members of the society in the British Isles and North America.

OAM is a training order for the Ophidian Traditional Craft, a serpent-venerating craft. This is an ancient craft – one of its magical texts, the Oera Linda Book, has sections that are over 4,000 years old. This book was compiled over several centuries by the Frisians, a nation who in historical times lived around the southern coast of the North Sea and what is now the Netherlands. These people believed that their ancestors had constructed the stone circles and megalithic monuments that still exist today in Europe. They also claimed to be descendants from the lost island of Atlantis.

The Frisians venerated Mother Earth as the most powerful

goddess and the World Serpent (Wr-alda) who fertilised Mother Earth with his life force. Together they produced three daughters (Lyda, Finda, and Frya), and the Frisians regarded these as the mothers of the human race. Frya was perfect, compared to her siblings, and was believed to have founded the Frisian civilisation. When Wr-alda came to Earth, this event marked the 'Cosmic Year' (Anno Mundi) of myth, the year when the 'King of the Cosmos' (Rex Mundi) returned. The Frisians were the ancestors of the Water Witches, the Canal Folk of the English Midlands. The Water Witches were a community of travellers who lived and worked on the canals and rivers in England until commercial canal-carrying ceased in 1970. They believed water to be the most important element, and that in its depths dwell ancient gods. Water is the physical manifestation of the World Serpent, and is therefore seen as the most magical of elements. OAM states:

> The Water Witches believed that after death we cease to exist. The only way of preventing this was to create a shade of oneself, which after death would go and inhabit one of the hells (though it could be summoned to Earth). This shade is then enabled to continue to exist by its living descendants regularly giving it new infusions of energy. Hell, therefore, is a desirable place to go after death, as the alternative is oblivion. Theoretically, one shade could successively inhabit an unlimited number of living bodies. Whether the shade exists in hell, or inhabits a living body, in both cases it is acting as a Vampire, taking energy that does not rightfully belong to it, and is thus dependent on the living.

Today the Ophidian Traditional Craft is preserved and passed on by the Ordo Anno Mundi to all of its initiates. A central tenet of the Ophidian Craft is the veneration of ancestors and therefore many rituals involve the summoning of ancestors to physical manifestation. OAM explains: 'Hence the spirits of the dead survive by regular infusions of the life force from those still living and in this sense their nature is vampiric.'

Ophidians have another connection with the legend of vampires in the form of shape-shifting. This is another ancient practice and allows a person to transform into the semblance of a creature, either real or imaginary, and thereby possess the abilities of that creature. According to OAM, this is the origin of the stories of witches (and their eastern European counterparts, vampires) being able to turn themselves into bats or wolves. A spokesperson for OAM has stated:

> Shape-shifting – and animal-shifting – has been around for generations and is widely practised around the world today. It is too deep to just come in without prior teaching and practice. I know for a fact that strange things happen and the first time I ever experienced such a thing myself was when I had 'wild dreams' of being a wolf and that I could actually smell the ground and see it as running on all fours. It was a unique and terrifying experience. All my senses were heightened to a degree that I've never found since. Running through dew and wet grass was exciting and it was a hunt and all was to a point, even when I felt pain in 'my paw'. The morning after my dream, I suddenly remembered and it was so eerie. When I got up, my right foot was bruised and swollen and my toe cut, with blood all over the sheets. What is real and what is not?

Like most branches of the Traditional Craft, the Ophidian Traditional Craft has seven initiatory degrees. The Outer Mysteries consists of the first three degrees. After filling in a membership form, new members begin their magical training and complete the first three degrees: 'Witchcraft and Sorcery' (evocation, spell-casting, ritual and divination); 'Pure Invocation' (summoning of nature spirits, deities and other entities) and 'Transcending the Physical Body' (astral projection, visiting other planes of existence). After the first year, when the trainee has reached Second Degree, they are encouraged to set up a new OAM Coven as an integral part of their own magical development. The trainee is now ready to be admitted into the Inner Mysteries: 'Werewolf or Animal Transformation' (shape-shifting, magical continence, non-human powers): 'Core Tradition Elements' (Traditional magical lore and techniques); 'Senate of the Order' (membership of the general assembly) and finally the 'Vault of the Order' (membership of the governing committee). Supposedly the final stages allows one to be eligible for the position of king or queen. Although there are seven official degrees, the eighth can be seen as close as one can be to a vampire. Each level and degree of initiation of Traditional Witchcraft of the Ordo Anno Mundi, involves a certain amount of 'secret knowledge' being imparted to the initiate. The OAM has a policy of secrecy and privacy and in the membership application form, members must agree never to reveal any OAM teachings to an outsider.

The internet has enhanced communications for trainees. Whereas beforehand members received their training by post, email is now used. A one-off payment of £50 entitles the member to life membership. All members can then access a special encrypted members' site for chats with other members. Many members from around the world come together and form a Temple Coven to carry out rituals together. Others make a pilgrimage to the Order's headquarters or other Temple Covens to meet and work. OAM states:

> Anyone can learn something of their magickal powers. The ancient arts and spells are there to be rediscovered, given patience, common sense and a longing to know. You can heal yourself, gain peace from stress of modern-day living and find ways of coping with the constant turmoil of living in the 21st century. You can protect yourself from psychic vampires, those that constantly want your help and attention and wear you down. To obtain all this and more, one must become dedicated and be willing to work and struggle, practise and practise even more. Discipline to be able to do all this will come as one sees more and more successes and strange coincidences that comply with one's inner wishes happen in their lives. No one can simply pass on power and it certainly cannot be bought. Magic itself is a neutral force, like electricity or magnetism, and can be used for any purpose whatever. This must not be interpreted as a 'Do whatever you want!' system. Experience teaches us that negativity breeds more negativity, so is best avoided. The OAM takes a very dim view of any member who brings the Craft into disrepute, either by abusing their position, or using magic for immoral purposes. Such people will be expelled.

Many vampires practise a mystical form of spirituality based on their vampiric status. Some forms of Vampyre Magick include Sangomancy and VampyreCraft. Sangomancy is a path of mixing blood and chaos magick. VampyreCraft is the magic practised by psychic or sanguine vampires who are Wiccans/witches or Neo-Pagan practitioners of magick. Vampyrcraft is often characterised by a balance between dark and light techniques and practitioners seek to balance the dark and light aspects within themselves. The Sanguinarium says of VampyreCraft: 'In general, this is the magick practised by vampyres. Many vampyres are pagan and follow the old ways, and the ways of magick are an integral part of their beliefs. Most vampyres practice numerous techniques associated with energy manipulation.'

Many vampires are drawn to worship gods and goddesses connected with the underworld, such as Lilith, the Dark Mother Goddess and spiritual forebear for many VampyreCraft practitioners. Lilith is considered the original vampire. According to Hebrew tradition she was Adam's first wife and was cast from the Garden for refusing to submit to him. Thus God cursed her with a thirst for blood, and she produced demonic children. Lilith and her heirs were believed to feed upon infants and young men, drinking their blood. However, today the modern philosophy of the Lilith tradition is a positive one; many practitioners acknowledge Lilith as a strong female figure and worship her as a patron goddess no longer affiliated with the death of children and the source of destruction. Many Lilians drink blood and also incorporate blood into their ritual. In the Bible, Cain – the son of Adam and Eve – killed his brother Abel and was thus the first murderer. In vampire lore some people believe Cain is the Father of Vampyres as God sent him out to wander in the world, cursing him with immortality. Cain is often linked to Lilith, as both were cast out of the Garden of Eden. Cainites, people who follow Cain, drink blood, although they also supplement this with life energy.

Vampirism as a religion is growing. Bholanath, spokesperson for the Order of the Crimson Tongues, says:

> My personal prediction is that vampyrism (or at least an expressed interest in it) will eventually replace LeVay's Satanism as the pathway for disenfranchised and disgruntled youth. As 'V Book I: Liber Jahira: The Black Veil' and 'V Book III: Liber Calmae: Sanguinomicon' get picked up by major distributors, I expect them to eventually become even more popular than *The Satanic Bible* or *Satanic Rituals.*'

Most of these vampire religions are based in America. One can only wait and watch to see if similar churches and temples will one day operate in the UK. Mick of the London Vampyre Group explains:

> I have often read that the reason why the US is such a religious society is that Britain encouraged most of its religious fundamentalists to go there in the 17th and 18th centuries (e.g. the Puritans and Pilgrim Fathers). The result is that Britain became more free thinking and the US became an uptight society. Organising as temples/churches, or its inverse, covens/lodges seems to an outside observer to be a logical way for communities to organise in the US with the attendant religiosities and types of structure, with fathers, sisters, priests, etc., a natural

consequence. We may yet get vampire temples, but that sort of energy seems to be going in the direction of the pagan alternative, which is becoming quite popular now.

Indeed, there can be no surprise that vampirism is often intertwined with religion. Western tradition presents a paradox by simultaneously perverting and reinforcing the images and rituals of Christianity. Blood communion, death and resurrection are central to both the Christian faith and vampire belief. Perhaps Stoker deliberately chose Vlad the Impaler as the model for Dracula for religious reasons, bestowing his creation with a god-like status. In 1431 Vlad joined the Order of the Dragon and thanks to the Vatican's support he gained the throne. In his book Vampires or Gods, William Meyers notes: 'There are persistent rumours that the real Vlad Dracula did not die in 1476. Instead he became an important figure in the Catholic Church, and an effective director of the Inquisition, which was directed primarily against Jews, Protestants and the growing rationalism of the scientists.'

Vampire conspiracists might add that the body of Vlad has never been found ...

CHAPTER 13

COUNTESS ELIZABETH –
INSIDE A VAMPIRE COVEN

'We live, We are, We feed.'

This is the tenet of the Countess Elizabeth's Vampire Coven, a real vampire club in the south of England. The coven was formed in 2003 and is the only one of its kind in the UK. Such covens, as we have discovered in previous chapters, are not uncommon in the USA and have been operating there for many years.

Countess Elizabeth's Vampire Coven (CEVC) is influenced by several American real vampire groups including House of Sanguinarium, House Khephru and Order Strigol. CEVC follow The Black Veil and the vampire codex, however they use them as guidelines only as they have combined them with their own code of ethics, specific to their own coven. The Black Veil can be viewed at the end of this chapter.

CEVC maintain they are real vampires, who believe in the occult system of dark magic, alchemy and ritual. Father Ruthven explains:

We believe in the secrecy of the lifestyle and of the people involved. We follow The Black Veil and the codex wherever possible, we offer our own teachings but do not dispute the knowledge of the other houses/clans/sects/orders. We amalgamate shared knowledge into our own experiences and opinions. we believe vampirism and the occult are closely linked and we combine the two philosophies in an easy-to-digest modern method. We want awareness for our kind in a media friendly way, secrecy is penultimate. We hope to help others embrace what they truly are, teach them the path and give support in any way we can. We are all family, and respect everyone within. Together we can achieve more than our wildest imaginings.

Our aim is to teach, help, advise and provide security for all those awakening as well as providing social evenings and events, encouraging everyone to mix and build relations. We are a large family after all and should try to be as close to one another as possible. We aim to dispel the myths relating to our kind, through example and knowledge. Far too many of us know our path but choose not to follow it. With guidance and support we aim to show the path and help follow it always, this is never easy but with such a large family, help is forever near. Know who you are and maintain it. We all have to alter our image at times but little discreet touches can provide constant support. If you have a day job, the house or coven sigils worn around your neck (even underneath clothes) can provide comfort.

Primarily due to the lack of similar organisations of their American counterparts, Father Ruthven and Countess Elizabeth decided to form their own group. They explain:

We felt there was nothing like our group in England as they all seem to be focused in America. We have attended some London vampire meetings, like the Vampyre ConneXion. However, most of these groups are simply fans of vampire movies getting together. There is no harm in that, but very few express interest in real vampirism. Our aim is to teach, help and inform others about real vampirism. However we cannot at the moment have too many people joining as we need to grow within the clan first. Presently we feel we have space for 200 members. Our ethos is different as all houses will say we agree with the guidelines placed by the leading elders, but being individuals we add our own guidelines or methods based on personal opinion.

Both myself and the Countess have been students of the occult for many years. We have always felt we were vampires. Through the study of the ancient tomes, the few still commercially available, we were able to learn more. During my study of alchemy and necromancy, I came across a now disbanded group of Victorian aristocrats, who claimed to possess the secret of vampirism. They were called the Order of the Blood Adepti. This disbanded group of Victorian aristocrats died in 1876. They have been linked to the infamous Hellfire Club. The Order of the Blood Adepti practise many occult traditions, the most important being: necromancy, alchemy, black magic and divination. We are currently correlating our information to create a clear history. Our purpose is to offer a haven for vampires to share with others of the experience. Vampirism is about the inherent ability to acquire unique and needed energy resources. There are those who draw their strength or energy from pranic sources or direct life giving sources such as blood and sexual energy. There are psychic vampires who seek and are able to use the energy of the Earth around them such as storms and other natural events or even living things. But the vampire is a predator and an energy feeder like no other. The coven continues to grow in strength as more true vampires find the haven they seek with others. We must be able to cope with the misconceptions brought on by media and the film industry.

All potential members of the coven must be over 18 years of age. They are initially asked to complete a questionnaire with queries such as: 'Do you feel different about yourself?' Do you feel you do not belong in this world? Have you ever tasted human blood? Do you feel more awake at night? Why do you want to join a serious vampire group? Do you think you could study and learn about vampires?

Discretion is key and the coven offer to reply to members via a secret envelope if desired. Membership to the coven costs £15 per month and this entitles the member to a weekly newsletter, a T-shirt with the coven sigil, and access to bars and clubs. There is also a monthly meeting with free refreshment. All new members receive a pewter medallion in the shape of a coffin and they must wear these while attending meetings. Indeed, members not wearing the medallion are not admitted to events. This is a similar procedure to the Sanguinarium, who identify themselves by another item of jewellery, an ankh.

Members also receive free a special CEVC T-shirt and a hand-crafted sigil of the vampiric soul from Abramelin the Mage, although this is also free to non members for the price of £15. There is also available to purchase the Blood Bible, a tome of knowledge featuring all the essays, teachings and codes of the Order of the Blood Adepti. CEVC produce a newsletter available every week.

That members receive a sigil devoted to Abramelin the Mage is significant. And who was Abramelin the Mage? Abramelin is a mysterious figure in history, and the little that is known of him has seen held him in high regard in modern occultism. Abramelin was an Egyptian sage and knowledge of him comes from a medieval manuscript based on an original Hebrew manuscript and titled 'The Book of the Sacred Magic of Abramelin the Mage, as delivered by Abraham the Jew unto his son Lamech, AD 1458'. This work details the complete system of magic of Abramelin and is considered a classic text in modern occult circles; Aleister Crowley, among others, held the book in high esteem. 'The Book of the Sacred Magic' details necessary qualifications to learn the Sacred Magic of Abramelin, of which there are two essential parts. Firstly, there is the invocation and conversation with the Holy Guardian Angel, which opens the path of communication between man and the divine. Secondly, there is the evocation of evil demons, which the magician learns to conquer and command to do his bidding by force of will and magic. Hence, once the magician has mastered this evocation of good and evil spirits, he can command those spirits to do his will. The last part of this book gives specific instructions for clairvoyance, divining metals and treasure, warding off evil magic, healing illness, levitation, transportation, making oneself invisible, creating illusions, reading minds, and other powers and magics, both white and black, which the magician may now utilise.

The philosophy of CEVC is that of an ancient occult belief of study, teaching and practice. The coven is made up of 13 clans, to 'link the entire UK with the dark brotherhood'. Following interviews, each member is selected by the elders and is placed into houses according to their strengths and weaknesses. The coven has limited membership available, to rebuild the other clans from the ashes and 'succeed where our past brothers failed'.

The first house is the magus clan and is the priest chaste responsible for all ritual ceremonies and the teaching of the blood code. The second house is the wamphyrie clan, who are responsible for the media and the protection of all members of the order and also all the teachings of the Blood Adepti. The third house is the house of the clan elders, which runs the coven. This is the largest chaste and is the central meeting point for the leaders of the other clans. According to their doctrine, entitled 'Blood Faith':

We celebrate six ersbats and five sabbats, the most important to us is the feast of Walpurgis. Entrance to the sacred temple is restricted to high ranking members of the magus clan only. A list of rituals, spells will follow shortly. Look to the faith always.

Like most real vampire organisations and individuals, issues of health and safety are of paramount concern to CEVC. They are anxious not to endanger their own health or that of their donors and stress the importance of minimising any risks:

Blood donors are advised to exercise caution, study relevant sections on their website and if certain they wish to proceed, use a registered donor. The donors especially because they need to provide a health check certificate, as diseases like AIDS are a very real risk. We only ask this of our donors as it is very important for the safety of the members. We ask the members to do this if they wish to have a donor from our list only not if they have their own. That would be an invasion of their rights. With piercings it is simply asked that they are kept clean to normal hygiene standards. Some people may think this is strange, but we cannot afford a scare in the community. The bad press that would follow would be very destructive.

We ask donors to go to the local sexual health clinic where you can have a complete test for free. The donors put themselves on a list and a member will contact them. We have strict guidelines for feeding which are always adhered to. The member will then meet the donor and it will then be a mutual decision. If for any reason the donor feels they have been victimised in any way we expel the member after due investigation. If the member is in any way criminal in his/her actions the police are informed. We have a lecture on feeding guidelines on the website. It is just a possible scenario we would like to avoid. We have not expelled anyone but there are procedures should the need arise.

The coven provide several sources as essential reading matter. One essay is titled 'What do you mean by a real vampire?' written by Inanna Arthen, and states:

Real vampires have vampire souls. They are born this way, they cannot change and the powerful nature of their vampiric aspect will come out whether they ever acknowledge it consciously or not. If they do not acknowledge it, they will often have miserable lives. If they do, they find themselves feeling lonely and isolated by the secret awareness of how different they are and by the fact that very few humans will believe in them.

According to this viewpoint, psychic vampires do not exist and the concept of psychic vampirism was simply popularised among occultists beginning in the 19th century. Real vampires, of course, have been around far longer. Arthen continues:

Vampires are vampires. All real vampires are psychic vampires by nature. All real vampires should also be drinking blood or getting other material sources of pranic energy, because they have material bodies. There is no distinction among blood-drinking vampires and psychic vampires. Any real vampire who has evolved a blood-drinking practise is a psychic vampire, whose imbalances are being controlled by regular intake of blood. Under certain circumstances, ordinary humans may become so exhausted, emotionally needy or imbalanced that they begin to draw energy from those close to them, leaving their lovers, housemates or friends feeling drained and ill. This is a temporary and correctable condition, and it would be unconstructive and cruel to label such people 'psychic vampires', no matter how difficult they might be to deal with. They are people who need help. Real vampires cannot change their nature.

For many, the drinking of blood signifies the true sign of a real vampire. But CEVC acknowledges that many real vampires do not drink blood. Sometimes this is through choice and other times it is a reaction to social conditioning. Although blood is believed to be the most concentrated material source of life force, it is not the exclusive one. Real vampires can learn to excel at absorbing pranic energy from around them and adapt their diet accordingly. For example, certain foods contain high levels of pranic energy like leafy fresh vegetables, seeds, nuts and beans. Indeed, some real vampires become vegetarians in order to maximise the pranic energy content in their diet. And what about the myth of bloody meat? According to the CEVC website, 'Commercially purchased meat has almost none, due to the "ageing" process in which the meat is partially decomposed to make it more tender.'

Although scientific argument shuns the human body's ability to digest blood, real vampires are exempt and can directly utilise the pranic energy content of blood. Whereas the normal human will vomit at the emetic properties of blood when ingested in large quantities, real vampires have developed a tolerance to blood.

In an essay on the site, Father Ruthven of the CEVC puts forward an argument for past-life memory recall. He believes that all vampires who remember a name or a building from the past could in fact be recalling their past vampire lives. Humans only use a small percentage of their brains, the rest is likened to a massive archive facility where past lives are stored. He explains:

We do not know if immortal vampires exist, there is no proof either way. My theory is that immortal vampires inject their essence into us thereby gaining a new body, where they store their collective memory. These past lives that we as vampires recall could be the memory of past vampires. That is why we can see and feel them so vividly. Most of us will wear a specific style or do something because it brings some kind of familiarity. That feeling may not be related to our current memories but our past life ones. For example, I have lived two past lives so far that my training will allow me to see. In the first I am a Victorian poet, a bit of a dandy, dabbling in the black arts and all I know is that people were afraid of me. The second I am an Egyptian priest writing and keeping scrolls. This has undoubtedly affected who I am today. I like Victorian clothes, love books and write poetry, more than just a coincidence. A few of my brethren have told me similar dreams – in their dreams they appear to be flying and some notice rats or bats, even fog. I suppose a theory that perhaps their past-life recall was trying to say they were vampires in their past life and the 20th-century part of our brain interprets those images as the cliché that vampires can fly, change into bats and all the usual Hollywood interpretations.

Could it be that Countess Elizabeth's Vampire Coven have made contact with the disbanded group of Victorian aristocrats, who claimed to possess the secret of vampirism? Perhaps Father Ruthven and Countess Elizabeth have found these very people who were been linked to the infamous

Hellfire Club, the notorious gentlemen's club famed for its depravity, and devil worship, with members drawn from the cream of the political, artistic and literary establishments, who dedicated themselves to Satan. Indeed, perhaps the informal network of Hellfire Clubs that once thrived in Britain during the 18th century, dedicated to debauchery and blasphemy, is set to rise again – with vampires at its helm.

THE BLACK VEIL

The Black Veil, also known as the '13 Rules of the Community', was composed by Father Todd of House Sahjaza, Michelle Belanger of House Kheperu and COVICA as a voluntary standard of common sense, etiquette and ideals for the greater vampyre/vampire community. Although copyright 1997–2001 by Father Todd and Michelle Belanger, The Black Veil is an open licensed text available for reproduction on related websites or in print for organisations and individuals who wish to promote its concepts and ideals. All that is asked is that the Black Veil not be changed, amended or modified in ANY way.

1. DISCRETION

This lifestyle is private and sacred. Respect it as such. Use discretion in who you reveal yourself to, and make certain that your motives are to truly communicate about our culture and to engender understanding. By no means should you talk to others about yourself and our community when your motives are for selfish reasons such as self-promotion, sensationalism, and attention-getting.

Do not hide from your nature, but never show it off to those who won't understand.

2. DIVERSITY

Our paths are many, even though the journey we are on is essentially the same. No single one of us has all the answers to who and what we are. Respect everyone's personal views and practices. We cannot let petty differences of ideology prevent us from maintaining a unified community; there are enough who would attack us from the outside.Our diversity is our strength. Let our differences in viewpoint enrich us but never divide us upon ourselves.

3. SAFETY

Use sense when indulging your nature. Do not flaunt what you are in public places. Feed in private and make certain your donors will be discreet about what happens between you. Donors who create rumours and gossip about us are more harm than they're worth. If you engage in blood-letting, put safety and caution above all other things. Blood-borne diseases are a very real thing, and we cannot risk endangering ourselves or others through irresponsibility. Screen donors carefully, making certain they are in good health both mentally and physically.

Never overindulge or get careless. The safety of the entire community rests upon each member's caution.

4. CONTROL

We cannot and should not deny the darkness within. Yet we should not allow it to control us. If our beast or shadow or darkside is given too much sway, it clouds our judgment, making us a danger even to those we love. Never indulge in pointless violence. Never bring willful harm to those who sustain you. Never feed only for the sake of feeding, and never give over to mindless blood lust. We are not monsters:

we are capable of rational thought and self-control.Celebrate the darkness and let it empower you, but never let it enslave your will.

5. LIFESTYLE

Live your life as an example to others in the community. We are privileged to be what we are, but power should be accompanied by responsibility and dignity. Explore and make use of your vampire nature, but keep it in balance with material demands. Remember: we may be vampires, but we are still a part of this world. We must live lives like everyone else here, holding jobs, keeping homes, and getting along with our neighbors. Being what we are is not an excuse to not participate in this reality. Rather, it is an obligation to make it a better place for us to be.

6. FAMILY

We are, all of us, a family, and like all families, various members will not always get along. However, respect the greater community when having your disputes. Do not let your individual problems bring emotional strife to the family as a whole. Settle your differences quietly among one another, only seeking out an elder's aid in mediation when no other solution seems possible. Never bring your private disputes into public places and never draw other family members into the issue by forcing them to take sides. Like any normal family, we should always make an effort to present a stable and unified face to the rest of the world even when things are not perfect between us.

7. HAVENS

Our havens are safeplaces where everyone in the community can come to socialize. There are also often public places where we are likely to encounter people who don't understand our ways. We should respect the patrons of these places as we should also respect the owners of the establishments and always be discreet in our behavior. We should never bring private disputes into a haven. We should never initiate violence in a haven. And we should never do or bring anything illegal into a haven, as this reflects badly upon the community as a whole. The haven is the hub of the whole community, and we should respect it as such, supporting it without business and working to improve its name in the scene so that we can always call it home.

8. TERRITORY

The community is extensive and diverse. Every city has a different way of doing things, and a different hierarchy of rule. When entering a new city, you should familiarize yourself with the local community. Seek out the local havens. Learn what households have sway here. Get in touch with key members of the community, learn who is who, and show proper respect where it is due. You should not expect to impose your old way of doing things on this new scene. Rather you should adapt to their rules and be glad of their acceptance. Always be on your best behavior when coming to a new city either to visit or to stay. We are all cautious and territorial by nature, and only by making the most positive impression possible will you be accepted and respected in a new community.

9. RESPONSIBILITY

This lifestyle is not for everyone. Take care in who you choose to bring into it. Those who are mentally or emotionally unstable have no place among us. They are dangerous and unreliable and may betray us in the future. Make certain that those you choose to bring in are mature enough for this burden. Teach them control and discretion, and make certain that they respect our ways. You will be responsible for their actions, and their behavior in the community will be reflected back to you.

10. ELDERS

There are certain members of our community who have established themselves as just and responsible leaders. These are the people who helped establish local communities, who organize havens, and who work to coordinate the networking of the scene. While their word does not have to be law, they should nevertheless be respected. They have greater experience than many others, and usually greater wisdom. Seek these elders out to settle your disputes, to give you guidance and instruction, and to help you establish yourself in the local scene. Appreciate the elders for all they have given you: if it was not for their dedication, the community would not exist as it does now.

11. DONORS

Without those who offer themselves body and soul to us, we would be nothing. We cannot be other than what we are, but it is the donors who sustain our nature. For this service, they should be respected. Never mistreat your donors, physically or emotionally. They are not to be manipulated or leeched off of for more than what they freely offer. Never take them for granted. Appreciate them for the companionship and acceptance which they offer us, which so many others would refuse. This above all: appreciate the gift of their life. That communion is sacred. Never fail to treat it as such.

12. LEADERSHIP

When you choose to take a position of authority in the community, remember that you do not lead for yourself alone. Leadership is a responsibility, not a privilege. A good leader must set an example for everyone through his actions and behavior. His motives should be selfless and pure, and he should put the interests of the whole community before his own.

The best leaders are those who serve to better the community and whose person and behavior gives no one – even those outside of the community – a reason to criticize them.

13. IDEALS

Being a vampire is not just about feeding upon life. That is what we do, but not necessarily what we are. It is our place to represent darkness in a world blinded by light. We are about being different and accepting that difference as something that empowers us and makes us unique. We are about accepting the dark within ourselves and embracing that darkness to make us whole beings. We are about celebrating the thresholds: body and spirit, pleasure and pain, death and life. Our lives should be lived as a message to the world about the beauty of accepting the whole self, of living without guilt and without shame, and celebrating the unique and beautiful essence of every single soul.

CHAPTER 14

VAMPIRE WARS – VAMPIRE HATERS AND SLAYERS

Not everybody loves a vampire. Some people positively hate them. At the one end of the spectrum are the relatively harmless 'haters' and at the other end are the real life vampire hunters. While vampires inspire passion in aficionados, it is also true that there are people with a definite grudge against them. Whether it is a case of dislike, scorn, pity or hate, vampires have their enemies. Hating vampires is one thing, but killing them? Indeed, proclaimed vampires do indeed face such levels of contempt and for this very reason they shroud their identities in secrecy. Most modern-day vampire hunters may not stalk their victims with a pointed stake, but they have the same contempt for their nemesis as any real-life vampire slayer. Harmless hunters who do not seek out vampires or commit any criminal activities include groups like The Dr Van Helsing Society.

Blood-drinking vampires hate psi vampires, Goths scorn vampires, rival vampire societies hate each other, Goths hate vampire role players. Between different categories of vampires themselves, there is friction – and even hate. Many sanguine vampires scorn psychic vampires because technically psychic vampires can 'feed' without consent – that is, they can take energy from subjects without asking permission. Of course, it is much harder for a sanguine vampire to do this, as people are more likely to notice someone stealing their blood as opposed to their energy! Hence, many sanguine vampires view psychic vampires' taking of energy as outrageous as theft and even rape. In their eyes, psychic vampires face greater moral dilemmas as the temptations to abuse psychic abilities are far greater than the temptations for those who drink blood.

Real vampires usually receive a one-sided press. Whether in films, books, television, or newspapers, the vampire is forever the murdering monster. In reality, vampires pose practically no harm to society in general, apart from in extreme cases. It is precisely because these incidents are so rare that they make headlines in newspapers and news bulletins. Certainly the number of vampire crimes reported in the UK each year is minute compared to other crimes such as murder, robbery and assault.

'Stop Vampire Hate on the Net' by the Real Vampire Coalition is a site dedicated to preventing hatred of vampires on online forums and notice boards through education and awareness. The site was set up to balance the negative press that vampires attract and allow vampires to speak out and defend themselves. The site declares in its mission statement:

> This site was started because I know what it's like. I was hurt for being a vampire. And if that wasn't bad enough, I go online, surfing with my cousin and see an anti-vampire board ... With hunters posting on it

... It made me sick ... My cousin said it's just a board by some role players, but the more I looked into it, the more I saw some of these people were real hunters out to get real vampires. The violence has to stop folks. Some have been hurt and scared. And some wonder why we hide what we are. Because we are afraid to be hurt. And to those hunters snooping around the page – we will no longer let you threaten and insult us. We have rights, no matter how much you hate that.

Why do people wish to destroy vampires? Perhaps people do not understand real vampires. Most people think vampires are immortal, beautiful, powerful creatures, or evil red-eyed monsters with long nails and fangs. OH PLEASE! We are NOT immortal. The Haters, why do they hate us? Is it because they do not understand? Or that they are just plain ignorant? Some hate because they do not understand us, yet they really don't try to. If they did, they would understand that we vampires have donors and don't walk up to a person and attack them! And not all vampires are blood drinkers. Some are psychic vampires. Haters hate because they do not understand the meaning of what it is to be a vampire, and if they do, maybe they are really screwed up or suffer some type of mental illness. No offence to them, just I can not see why you hunt us. Some 'hunters' or haters may hunt us just because we are 'Evil' due to their religion. Religion in my personal opinion can play a factor for the vampires haters in the world. Religion is both good and bad, some religious people take it too far and become 'vampire hunters'. Remember folks, bibles and books are just words and guidelines. And when hunters do stalk their 'prey', they hurt a person who has a family just like them, who has a job like them, who has a life just like them.

The people behind Stop the Vampire Hate work towards 'The Dream' – i.e. the end of hate for vampires both on the net and in the real world. The dream can only be achieved by spreading proper information that will increase the general public's understanding of vampires:

Surfing the net and finding a message board where real vampire 'hunters' post and talk about finding one, and how their friend will bring the gun to kill them is just plain sick! But online we need a break, maybe to get away from the hate... A chance to talk to other vampires without fear with meeting some nut that wants to kill us! It's pretty sad if a 'hunter' poses as a vampire and talks another real vampire into meeting him or her... The vampire could be killed, stalked, or whatever... That's not right... By any standards of morals... All we want is to be left in peace... a chance to exist on the net without the hate.

'How can I become a vampire slayer?' Surprisingly, this is a question that many vampire sites often receive. Surely real vampires would not give out this advice, and if these would-be hunters had any sense they would direct their enquiries to vampire hunter sites. Vampire sites often receive correspondence from hunters and programmes like *Buffy the Vampire Slayer* increased this type of correspondence. One vampire site that was receiving such correspondence responded:

I feel that this strange desire some people have to feel like they have a heroic mission to kill vampires should be addressed. Many people feel a powerful need to get out and do something important in the world, and for some of them, everyday good deeds just aren't enough. That's why *Buffy the Vampire Slayer* is so popular, and all the endless vampire stories in which the vampires are the bad guys and the heroes are the ones wielding the crosses and stakes. That's why people read super-hero comic books. But it's kids' stuff. Living vampires are no more likely (or unlikely) to be unethical or criminal than any random human, and they certainly aren't 'evil'. They're your fellow beings on this planet. Killing them is murder, plain and simple. And there's no justification for it. You're performing no great act of heroism by slaughtering another intelligent being, no matter how you rationalise it. You'll pay for it in this lifetime, by being caught and punished, and you'll pay for it karmically, as well.

But if you truly feel called to join the front lines, Fight the Good Fight, slug it out with the dark side of the Force, there's plenty of work out there for you to do. It's not as glamourous as slinking around in a trenchcoat with stakes and books full of esoteric knowledge, but it needs doing. You can fight racism in the inner city, train yourself for a career in law enforcement, become an environmental activist, become a priest or a Franciscan, volunteer in a shelter or a food pantry or a day care centre. There are hundreds of thankless, low-paying or unpaid jobs you can do to help humanity and battle 'evil'. There are millions of people living lives of desperation who could use your help. There are a thousand ways you can be one of the Good Guys. But slaying vampires isn't one of them. It's time for all you 'vampire slayers' to grow up and join the real world.

The Vampire Donor/Alliance too are aware of the dangers of hunters. When asked if they are worried about hunters, their response is: 'Damn right we are! So worried that it borders on paranoia. Most of the "slayers" out there are Buffy wannabees, but there are a few nutcases.' The Vampire Donor/Alliance do not shirk from expressing strong words of hate against vampire cults and lifestylers. When criticised for their stance, a spokesperson says:

> I am very outspoken regarding groups that I consider to be cults, or that I feel display cultlike behaviour including excessive mystification, extreme cliquishness and exclusion of outsiders, lockstep conformity, discouragement of independent thought and attitude, discouragement of questioning, alternating use of reward and punishment, encouragement of members to have no life outside of the group, and discouragement of scepticism on the part of outsiders. I was a member of a small cult when I was a teenager. My best friend was dating a man who thought he was God, and had followers. They were the best, and worst and most threatening, years of my life. I want to protect impressionable, vulnerable seekers from such groups. Currently there are several groups on my cult 'shit list'... let's call one xxxx- (They can't even get the alchemist's name right, and they don't know that this

figure had no vampiric origins prior to Hotel Transylvania by Chelsea Quinn Yarbro.) The xxxx is not a cult, but is staffed mainly xxxx members and is a little fruity – it's trying to be a real life Talamasca and it flatters itself with delusions of serious research, but the results aren't exactly posted widely outside of the xxx and xxxx own virtual forum.

Neither are scathing attacks confined to online groups. Traditional vampire lifestyle societies in the UK that celebrate only the academic and cinematic vampire are not immune to their share of vampire hate.

Despite repeatedly stating that they do not practise real vampirism, societies such as the London Vampyre Group (LVG) often receive hate mail. This is a genuine mail exchange from an American notice board:

Come, get me I am a vampire hunter and you mother fuckin vamps will die

ooh, we are frightened! too much tv again? LVG

ok meet me here tommorrow [a misspelt address in the good old USA given here] and we will fight for you vamps deserve to die

Hi there ol' xx, I do wonder how seriously I should take someone who cannot spell their own address – how old are you? fifteen? Hold on, I have just realised you are a North American. You may be excused your crass gullibility, then. Maybe a few words for you to look up there. LVG why don't you face me, you to scared?

Actually, we couldn't get the bus fare together for that meeting – why don't you just concentrate on getting your teacher to check your spelling before you mouth off next time? LVG

when can you get the bus fare? when you do come so I can kick your ass

Why do you want to be so vicious to my donkey? LVG

I don't have a probelm with your 'donkey' I got a probelm with you blood sucker I see you are still having problems with your grasp of spelling – you know it would help if you practised more on crosswords or 'scrabble'. Anyway, you have a problem with us – what is that exactly? LVG

you are bloodsuckers you kill to live

Time to get real I think. I believe that you are having trouble telling the difference between reality and fantasy. None of us think we are real 'vampires' who kill to live, as you say. We are merely creating a fictional environment in which we can live out parts of our imaginations. When you say you are a 'slayer' I believed that you were doing the same, i.e. acting out a chosen role. There's nothing wrong with that so long as you understand the limits of your role-play, and I did feel that we were both indulging on some boisterous banter and just for fun. However, there are things which make me not so certain. None of us actually kills to drink blood, and to my knowledge we would all agree that drinking blood is just trite and obvious. So for your enlightenment, if you are going to accuse us of killing you need to come up with your evidence. I am sure your server, AOL, which takes a high moral stand on what goes through its computer, would not like to get involved in libel actions ... Are you having a laugh or what? LVG

This interchange ended here. But the London Vampyre Group does not just face scorn from would-be slayers. Over the years they have incurred the wrath of religious fanatics. In their very own Spanish Inquisition, the group received this email in Spanish, translated here:

You are in the thrall of the path of darkness – you are all damned! You think we do not know of your existence, but you are mistaken. The hour of divine justice has arrived. You are only the darkness, but we are the light. The war has begun and in time will turn against you. You are history. But the Heavenly Father is the light.

The London Vampyre Group responded:

I can only say that we openly announce our existence and you must be stupid to think that we are being secretive. Unlike you, who do not announce who you are. If you are the light, maybe you should illuminate us with your existence and your name. If the war has begun, are you threatening us? Do you not know that the years when you could burn and kill people who did not accept your narrow views have now gone and people in the world are a lot wiser. You hide behind pious statements and historical lies and all I can suggest is that you either grow up, or just go away and live in the Middle Ages. The Spanish Inquisition is now dead, so long live truth and enlightenment.

Over the past few years there have been a growing number of reports of hostility between real vampires and lifestylers. Real vampires become angry when lifestylers attract (or seek) publicity in the media, which real vampires feel gives the entire vampire community a bad reputation. Real vampires are almost resistant to media opportunities and hence scorn the lifestylers, who make outrageous claims about their own vampire lives. Incidents of violence and legal disputes are commonplace between both parties.

One would expect the Goth scene, with its vampiric look of black clothes and chalked-out faces, would be sympathetic to vampires. Not so. There is much rivalry between the two scenes. This rift reached a peak during the annual Whitby Goth Weekend in Whitby in 1996. Several incidents caused a furore between both groups: an attack on a girl by a 'vampire' in the graveyard; a planned walk through a graveyard organised by a local vampire society and the behaviour of a group of vampire role players who staged a mock fight in the main event foyer. The organiser of the event was forced to issue this statement:

Everything was hunkydory between all parties concerned until the damage occurred in the graveyard in the 1996 festival. The church asked us not to go up there in future years. So we went to grave efforts to co-operate by hiring £500 worth of security to patrol the graveyard through the evenings of April 1997 weekend and appealing to punters through the 1997 info pack to respect the church's wishes. The organisers of Vamps And Tramps (having full knowledge of the above) decided to run a masquerade parade through the streets of Whitby and up to the church yard during their 1997 event. I called the main organiser and asked her to reconsider her plans and work with me to keep the church and Whitby folks happy. She refused saying no one was going to tell her what to do. Consequently the church took out a court injunction and the story hit the national press. In several newspapers I was named as the organiser of an event that was being threatened with court action – this was very upsetting and damaging to my reputation.

While we are on the topic let's talk about the press – here's another gripe: fact: I don't court media attention – I don't want or need it, the Vampire element do. Vamps and Tramps felt it necessary to hold a press conference and invite everyone from NME to MTV to it. I have never invited any journalists to my event. The reason I don't invite the press is because they're only interested in a sensational angle – and where do they get it from? The sad attention seeker who tells them he's 40 years old and has had his name changed by deed poll to Vlad the arsehole. It makes a mockery of what I am trying to achieve. My festival is purely about Gothic music and fashion. It 's not about Vampires like it's not about Punk or Elvis.

I also had a run in with a group of live role players who insisted on playing *Vampire: The Masquerade* in the foyer during the 1996 event. This dismayed me for two reasons: 1.

Live role-playing states in the rules that it shouldn't be played in public areas such as nightclubs and running up to people who are having a drink and minding their own business and saying 'You're a Vampire now' really is totally unacceptable. 2. The fact that this group of people felt they had to create their own entertainment for the whole evening when I had laid on three live bands and the best Goth DJs the UK has to offer surely illustrates that they were seeking something I was not willing to provide.

I also received a very disturbing letter after the 1996 event which outlined an unprovoked incident where a girl was bitten on the neck by a complete stranger in the graveyard leaving her extremely distressed and in need of medical attention. I'm sure that in this day and age I don't need to point out to anyone the dangers of biting people.

The biggest fact that people should understand is that this isn't some kind of one-woman moral crusade. After the 1996 event and the subsequent court injunction incident there was much discussion on the Goth/Vampire issue. I received many communications and spoke to many people in clubs around the country on the topic. The stand I took in 1997 wasn't an impulsive one – it was very much a considered decision. It was rapidly reaching the point that if I didn't disassociate the Whitby Goth Weekend from the vampires, local opinion would make it impossible for me to continue to run the event in Whitby.

I'd like to mention also an incident where a bloke wearing a Vampire Guild T-shirt was threatened by four other Goths who in the process mentioned my name. I'd like to categorically state that I don't advocate Vampire bashing, just like I don't advocate gay bashing.

So let's summarise. I haven't got a problem with societies that appreciate the art, literature and folklore surrounding vampires. I haven't even got a problem with people that wear fangs – what I have a problem with is the small section of the vampire fraternity that find it impossible to differentiate between fantasy and reality who insist on turning my event into a media circus. My event is for those with an appreciation of the Gothic scene and if this small number of people are unable to act sensibly and maturely, then I'd rather they didn't come. I'm not saying that all Vampires are banned, I'm merely saying that after many years of media ridicule, I'm working flat out to give Goth the image it rightfully deserves and then up pops some idiot with fake blood dripping out of his mouth spouting on about how he drinks a pint of blood for breakfast every day and all my efforts are wasted.

Of course, the vampire contingent hit back. They felt ostracised and were offended by the booth at the main event selling T-shirts bearing slogans like 'Vampires Suck'. Maria was one of the offended vampire contingent. She explains:

> Without the Gothic and pseudo-gothic trappings of vampire fandom, Goth would have died a swift death circa 1988. If it had even lasted that long. When the Goth contingent went to the local press and proclaimed vampire fans 'an embarrassment to Goths everywhere' (I don't think Goths need any help in embarrassment, especially not from vampire fans), they proceeded to claim that vampire fans desecrated the graveyard of St Mary's Church by burning black candles and littering the area. But neither excursion could be traced to Goths nor vampire fans.

Nonetheless, the rot had set in and the ensuing round of half-hearted slugging in the local press took in the local curate and a local councillor who took out an interdict against the Whitby Dracula Society's traditional candlelit procession through St Mary's Church grounds. They were prepared to allow fans to go up individually but if a chain of people formed, it would result in the police being called and the injunction being enforced. Maria claims:

> This put a dampener on the event as many people were looking forward to the procession. At most a few dozen hardcore fans would have struggled up the 199 steps in the dark and sat in the graveyard, contemplating the bay, the town and the Abbey and discussing Stoker's classic work of the supernatural. No black magic rituals, no blood drinking and probably not even any partying would have gone on as many at the event have strong feelings regarding the sanctity of burial grounds and respect for the dead. And as for the 'Vampires Suck' T-shirts, well only if they are asked nicely, darling.

Thee Vampire Guild stated in its fanzine 'Crimson' that the whole debacle was rather silly: 'If Goths hate vampires so much, why do they dress like them? Don't they realise the stereotypical Gothic image has evolved from Carroll Borland in *Mark of The Vampire*?' Events culminated in a Vampire Guild member being assaulted in Nottingham apparently for nothing more than their appearance. A statement was issued on behalf of several vampire societies that attempted to draw a truce. To this day, however, the rift has continued and most Goths dismiss self-styled 'vampires' as a completely separate subculture, rather than a subgroup of the Goth scene.

The incident at Whitby escalated and became the subject of heated arguments and debates in fanzines and societies throughout the country, and even had the effect of causing a new society to form. The Dr Van Helsing Society (DVHS) was founded by two Glaswegians, Brian and David, during a trip to the aforementioned Whitby Gothic festival. Although they did not seek to kill vampires, they publicly voiced their disgust at them:

> During the weekend vampire role-players came along and spoiled people's enjoyment, because they believe they are vampires and start all this stupid carry on. They had weapons and re-enacted a mock fight in the main event foyer. We decided to form the Society as a reaction against people like that who genuinely believe they are vampires.
>
> Because Whitby is synonymous with Dracula, you end up meeting people who really believe they are vampires so by the end of the weekend we had met quite a few. We heard a story about a man there who would not go into his hotel until he was invited in, like the supposed legend that a vampire cannot enter a room unless you invite it in. There are people who when they've been asked to fill in their registration card, put their dates of birth at two or three hundred years old. I don't mind people going under assumed names. But it's a different matter for people who genuinely believe that they are that person. That's when we started having difficulty, but then we thought no, we don't like people who pretend to be vampires either. That's when we crossed that line and started hating anyone that professed a love of

vampires. When we heard there was a Vampire Society in London a few years ago, we thought it was a drunken joke. Then when we found out it was real we thought that if there's a vampire society, why not a Doctor Van Helsing society? As a reaction against vampires. People like us have a place in society speaking out against vampires. The whole basis is that I don't personally like people who genuinely think they are vampires. People who are blood drinkers, we don't like. I personally don't entertain that. As both the DVHS and personally. If people can see that, that the DVHS is a joke with a sensible basis. We don't want people to think we're getting at anyone. I think the people who annoy me, annoy genuine vampire fans.

I think that everyone has got a thing; if it's vampires, and collecting vampire books, videos, dressing up – whatever. That's fine. I've got no problem with that at all. I was a member of the Vampire Guild but I didn't go as far as wearing fangs and thinking I was a vampire. People who wear fangs? It's not natural.

DVHS was also a reaction to an explosion of vampire fans in the nineties in Glasgow and when the local scene disbanded so too did the Dr Van Helsing Society. Interestingly the Society reflected the view of the moral majority, who agree that vampires are unwelcome visitors in the world: 'Let's not forget that in every vampire movie there is a hunter and in every vampire movie, we've won. In the majority of the Hammer films, the vampire gets killed. Dr Van Helsing always wins.'

It is no wonder that real vampires remain hidden from

society and hate like this only serves to bury them further underground and force them to evolve higher and higher codes of secrecy. Virtual vampire site Vampirecityuk pleads:

> I urge everyone in the vamp community to take care while in the public eye for too many have associated us with the objects of their hate. The law enforcement people have the power and bias to do us harm. We must both blend in and make wise choices in revealing ourselves to the public and media attention. We know their ignorance and prejudices, and must be wary of them. I also urge that we do not give up our individuality for it is our freedom of expression that establishes a large part of our identity. We are vampires and there is no changing that. We will remain a part of this world and nothing from anyone will change that.

THE TERROR THAT COMES IN THE NIGHT – EXTRATERRESTRIAL VAMPIRES

This book has been an investigation into vampires in the UK, with passing reference to vampires elsewhere in the world, particularly the USA. But there is perhaps somewhere else we have forgotten to look. The skies.

To find the modern real vampire, according to author Rosemary Ellen Guiley PhD, we must look not down into the earth but up into the skies. In her paper ' SEQ CHAPTER \h \r 1Vampires From Outer Space: An Exploration of Common Ground Shared by Vampires and Extraterrestrial', Guiley compares the core phenomena of vampire and extraterrestrial encounters and asserts they are almost identical: harassment, molestation, annoyance, assault, harm – and fear. Victims of vampire and extraterrestrial attacks both suffer similar outcomes: missing time, terrifying abductions, in which they are paralysed, where they are 'literally vampirized by sexual and physical assault'. Mysterious animal mutilations and deaths also have been blamed on vampiric ETs.

Guiley is a best-selling author of 30 books on paranormal, mystical, spiritual and visionary topics. She is an honorary fellow of the College of Human Sciences, the professional division of the International Institute for Integral Human Sciences in Montreal, Canada. Guiley puts forward an impressive argument and asks us to consider the similarities between vampires and extraterrestrials:

To see how blurry are the distinctions between vampires and ETs, can you tell which of the following anecdotes are about vampires and which are about ETs?

1. A girl has nightmares about a 'thing' that grabs her from behind. It has long, cold fingers that are thick at the ends.

2. A boy is visited every night at midnight by a 'thing' that steals up on him in bed. It paralyses him, suffocates him, and leaves him feeling exhausted the next day. Over time, his health declines and he becomes weaker.

3. A thing visits people at night, making noises and upsetting things in houses. It sexually molests people in their beds, and leaves bite marks and bruises upon their bodies.

4. A thing with 'devil's eyes' visits a woman at night. It paralyses her, squeezes her throat in a suffocating manner, pinches and bites her, and touches her in a sexual way. She awakens exhausted.

Example no.1 is a modern ET account from *Abduction: Human Encounters with Aliens* (1994) by John E. Mack, MD

. Example 2 is a vampire account, recorded in 1923 by Dr Franz Hartmann.

Example 3 is a vampire account from the 16th century in Breslau, Germany, recorded in 1868 by J. Grasse in a collection of Prussian folklore.

Example 4 is a modern ET account also from Mack's book.

Guiley concludes: 'The core phenomena are almost identical. These examples also can be compared in the same manner to a wide variety of cross-cultural accounts of unpleasant encounters with otherworldly beings. The hallmarks are harassment, molestation, annoyance, assault, harm – and fear.'

Although extraterrestrials have often been compared to other supernatural creatures, Guiley asserts that:

Little attention has been given to the similarities between ETs and vampires. These similarities are remarkable, and I believe the ET is closer to the vampire than other beings. Extraterrestrials and vampires share many characteristics in terms of their behaviour, phenomena associated with them, and their effects on the people and animals with whom they come into contact.

Other similarities between vampire and alleged extra-terrestrial encounters include the draining of blood from the body of the victim. Whereas vampires drain living beings of blood by puncturing the victim's skin, a similar blood loss occurred when waves of extraterrestrial attacks in South America in the seventies left people seriously ill, and even dead. The UFOs were nicknamed 'vampires in the sky'. Most of the victims were struck by mysterious beams of red light that severely burned their chests. Blood tests showed the victims to have abnormally low levels of haemoglobin. Some of the victims did not die directly from the burns, but suffered a wasting away over a period of months, and then died. Many people in the area believed that the ETs in the UFOs had come specifically to suck the blood or energy from people. They called the UFOs 'chupa-chupas', or 'suckers'.

Night-time presents the ideal opportunity for abduction, whether by a vampire or an extraterrestrial. At night victims are alone – moreover, the abduction can initially be mistaken as part of a dream. Both vampire and extraterrestrial encounters bear similarities to 'hag attacks'. The hag is a common figure in European folklore and is usually an ugly female that sits on her victim's chest. A hag attack is a type of molestation in which a demonic or alien entity visits and assaults an individual in bed. Victims of vampire or extraterrestrial encounters at night experience similar phenomena: victims awaken to a presence by their bed; they are 'paralysed'; they feel a weight on their chests. They are transported away, usually on a beam of light, to a UFO, where they are medically probed and perhaps sexually violated. During these assaults, they are unable to move and are terrified. In such cases, the ET is the modern version of the hag.

Folklorist David J. Hufford, an expert on the Old Hag syndrome, notes in *The Terror That Comes in the Night* (1982) that Bram Stoker was probably familiar with the characteristics of hag attacks and vampire folklore, as we see in this passage from Dracula, in which Mina describes a visitation by the Count:

> There was in the room the same thin white mist that I had before noticed… I felt the same vague terror which had come to me before and the same

sense of some presence... then indeed my heart sank within me: Beside the bed, as if he had stepped out of the mist – or rather as if the mist had turned into his figure, for it had entirely disappeared – stood a tall, thin man, all in black. I knew him at once from the description of the others. The waxen face; the high aquiline nose, on which the light fell in a thin white line; the parted red lips, with the sharp white teeth showing between; and the red eyes that I had seemed to see in the sunset on the windows of St Mary's church at Whitby... For an instant my heart stood still, and I would have screamed out, only that I was paralyzed.

Guiley explains:

Sleep and death have always been regarded as first cousins; sleep is often called 'the little death'. The dead are inherently vampiric. It is not surprising that entities embodying our deep fears of death come and assault us in our dreams. The dream has been recognised as a medium for visitations by otherworldly beings and the dead since ancient times. One could also be plagued by demonic or troubling beings who wished to molest the dreamer or suck off his life force. Anecdotal accounts exist of dream visitations by ghosts, poltergeists, vampires, demonic beings, nightmare hags, and witches, as well as helpful and benevolent beings such as angels, fairies, religious figures and spiritual guides. Visitations by the dead can be pleasant or unpleasant. Visitation dreams are distinctly different from ordinary dreams. They are intense and vivid in imagery, sensory experience and especially fear, and the dreamer is not certain of being awake or asleep. The dreamer may awaken certain that the 'dream' was a real event. Many ET dreams bear the same characteristics as other types of entity dream visitations: the sense of being 'real' and not a dream; fear; paralysis; inability to terminate the experience at will; some sort of molestation. These can be likened to modern-day vampire attacks. Today, we do not take 'real' vampires seriously, but we can take seriously vampiric encounters with space aliens, who come out of the darkness of the last frontier.

While the idea of vampires from space is not entirely new, no one has elaborated on it to the extent that Guiley has. As she notes:

The transference of a collective belief in vampires to the extraterrestrial encounter is a phenomenon with which we have yet to come to terms, due to conflicting beliefs about space aliens and arguments over their objective reality. When it comes to vampires, we remain preoccupied with the fictional creation, an increasingly beautiful creature clothed in lace with the sophisticated manners of High Court. These fictional vampires may be beautified and their evil neutralised, but, like their folklore counterparts, they reflect our deep concerns with eternal issues: fear of death, fear of darkness, and desire for eternal life and eternal youth. People tend to pigeon-hole things (aliens are this, vampires are that) and it's hard for them to see the murky area where they blend and come together. I think in the future, we're going to have to reorient our thinking about a lot of things.

So, are extraterrestrial vampires visiting us in our rooms at night? As I end this book, I ask you to think about that as you turn in at the end of your day.

Goodnight.

THE VAMPIRE IN CONTEMPORARY SOCIETY VIA A WORLDWIDE CENSUS

Thanks to a survey conducted by Dr Jeanne Keyes Youngson, assisted by Martin V. Riccardo and Jerome Miller, we can get an idea of just how far the vampire has insinuated itself into our culture. The purpose of the survey was not to investigate or analyse the causes for the recent explosion of interest in the genre, but rather to acknowledge that the phenomenon does exist, and also to tabulate data – statistics and other information resulting from questionnaires.

A total of 933 questionnaires were distributed inter-nationally between February 1998 and March 1999. 713 forms were returned. The form consisted of two sections. Part One was directed towards those who considered themselves to be 'vampires'. Part Two addressed those interested in the vampire genre, but who were not involved in a vampiric lifestyle.

Of the respondents, 91% were Caucasian, 3% Hispanic, 3% of mixed background, 2% African-American and 1% Asian; there were no Native-American respondents. North America provided 63% of respondents, 19% came from the UK and 18% from other countries combined. A total of 23 countries were represented in all.

Out of the 713 forms returned, 272 respondents claimed to be vampires, or to have been vampires in the past. A total of 441 non-vampires completed and returned Part Two. In all, 405 respondents were female and 308 were male; among them, there were three lesbians and two gay men among them.

Due to the complex nature of the survey, I have chosen to condense some lists, including those referencing occupations, hobbies, favourite books and movies. Those I have included are representative of the whole.

INTRODUCTION
By Martin V. Riccardo

It was in the 20th century that the vampire fully established itself as a universal archetype, one of the great mythic figures of modern times. Long before our present perception of the vampire took on its current form, the primal forces of the blood-sucking undead left a long and bloody trail through every century, even before the dawn of civilization. Prehistoric stone monuments known as dolmens have been found over the graves of the dead in northwest Europe. Anthropologists have speculated that these ancient stone structures may have been placed over graves to keep the dead from rising. Throughout the world, prehistoric graves have been found in which the bodies were buried with red clay ochre. Apparently the earliest peoples believed that something with the colour of blood could give new life to the dead.

Throughout the eras of civilization, people have feared dangerous ghosts, and supernatural beings that could drain blood. By the end of the Middle Ages, a belief developed in Eastern Europe that the dead could return, attack the living, and drink their blood.

This undead being went by many names, such as vukodlak, upir or vampire. By the 18th century, reports of these unearthly creatures in the East created a stir in Western Europe. Various scholars such as the French cleric Dom

Augustine Calmet, catalogued these weird accounts, and often tried to explain them.

Early in the 19th century, a popular interest developed in fictional vampires, spurred on by John Polidori's 'The Vampire' in 1819. At the end of the 19th century, Bram Stoker's novel *Dracula* made a profound impression on the public's perception of the vampire. Published in 1897, his novel combined the best elements of the Gothic novel with modern horror fiction. When we get to the early 20th century, we find that popular interest in the fictional Dracula is gradually increasing. By the 1920s, Stoker's story was transformed into a hit play in Britain and America. When the movie starring Bela Lugosi was released in 1931, the film's portrayal of Dracula influenced the way the entire world thought about vampires.

By the end of the 20th century, over 300 motion pictures were made about vampires, and over one hundred of them featured Dracula. In addition, over one thousand vampire novels were published in the 20th century, most of them in the last 25 years of this period. In the 1980s, vampire role-playing games gained popularity, and what is known as the Gothic music scene developed a strong and loyal following. By the 1990s, innumerable websites dealing with vampires appeared on the internet. There is no single answer as to why the vampire acquired this tremendous appeal in recent times, but it is obvious that this nocturnal creature incorporates feelings of dark romance, forbidden passion, immortality, danger, mystery, isolation and alienation. These and other aspects of the vampire, appeal to many people who often feel trapped in a cold, sterile, technology-led world.

One of the strangest developments in the last two decades of the 20th century is the significant number of people who have chosen to take on the characteristics, and sometimes the appearance of, the vampire. Many of these individuals are so drawn to the vampire that they even choose to identify themselves as such. While various attempts have been made to study these people, the efforts were often limited and incomplete.

For the end of the century we have Dr Jeanne Keyes Youngson to provide us with a full picture of the human vampire and vampire lover in our midst. Dr Youngson has been a leading figure in vampire research for more than a third of a century and thanks to her survey, we can get an idea of just how far the vampire has insinuated itself into our culture.

THE CENSUS
By Dr Jeanne Keyes Youngson

This is, of necessity, an abridged report of the final '20th Century Vampire Census'. Not only did an extraordinary number of people respond to the survey, but there were also unsolicited mailings from others touched by the power of the vampire mystique.

The following letter from a woman in Middle America is but one example of the many I received, especially after the publication of *Private Files of a Vampirologist* in 1997.

> For years now, in fact as far back as I can remember, I have been obsessed with Vampires. I have always felt that in some way I was supposed to be one. All of this is very confusing. I constantly feel I should be among vampires, but I do not know how to proceed.
>
> In addition and for some reason, I have always believed someone in my immediate family was either a vampire or was attacked by one.

What I really want to know is where I belong! I realise you get many letters from people who want to be vampires, but how many feel in their hearts, as I do, that actually being a vampire is their purpose in life? How many would be willing to sacrifice whatever is necessary to find the truth? I would be eternally grateful for any assistance you could offer.

Letters like this, which have been authenticated by experts such as Martin V. Riccardo, Eric Held, Norine Dresser and Elizabeth Miller, are yet another facet of the puzzling fascination the vampire figure holds for so many.

The purpose of the survey was not to investigate or analyse the causes for the recent explosion of interest in the genre, but rather to acknowledge that the phenomenon does exist and to tabulate data, i.e. statistics and other information resulting from questionnaires that were returned.

PART ONE

DO YOU THINK YOU ARE NOW, OR EVER
HAVE BEEN, A VAMPIRE?
Yes: 96%
No: 4%

DO YOU DRINK BLOOD?
Yes: 71%
No: 9%
Sometimes: 20%

IF YES, FROM WHOM OR HOW DO YOU GET IT?
Packaged raw meat; self; friend; lover; farm animals; spouse;
paid donors; slaughterhouse; willing donors; mixture of
friends' blood and red wine; anonymous donor in clubs; blood
exchange in clubs; licking cuts and other wounds.

   ALSO: Juices that resemble blood; tomato juice and six red
pepper flakes; beet juice and vinegar; warm Bloody Mary mix;
three drops of blood from my finger mixed with a shot glass of
Diet Coke.

DO YOUR FRIENDS KNOW YOU ARE A VAMPIRE?
Yes: 12%
No: 79%
A few: 9%

IS BEING A VAMPIRE A MATTER OF CHOICE FOR YOU?
Yes: 13%
No: 87%

DO YOU CONSIDER YOURSELF:
a) A true vampire?   41%
b) A psychic vampire?   23%
c) Vampire-like?   36%

DO YOU HAVE A VAMPIRE NAME?
Yes: 38%
No: 62%

IF YES, WHAT IS IT?
FEMALE: Dracula's Bride; Carmilla; Countess Noir; Claudia;
Orenthia; Black Beauty; Serpentine; Queen of the Dark;
Bloofer Lady; Sangrita; Lenore; Angelica; Lotus; Lady Death;
Willow; Dark Angel; Princess Moonbeam and EIGHT
Countess Draculas.
MALE: Dr Blut; Nosferatu; Latan Satar; Hawk; Thundergod;
Black Knight; Dante; Inn Keeper; Renaldo the Wolf; Lord Vlad;
Aristede; King of the Castle; Prince of Darkness; Lord Death;
Sir Sundown; Zorro; Wraith; Wolfman Jim; Dark Demon; two
Vlads and three Blades.

WERE YOU RAISED IN AN ORGANIZED RELIGION?
Yes: 69%
No: 31%

ARE YOU SENSITIVE TO ANY AROMAS?
Yes: 71%
No: 29%

IF YES, WHAT ARE THEY?
LIKES: Leather; lilacs; blood; burning leaves; musk perfumes;
aeroplane glue; rotting meat; the smell of Grandma's attic and

old houses; roses; new car interiors; 'whiteout'; pine trees and needles; sandlewood; cedar; incense; old books; fresh brewed coffee; chocolate.

DISLIKES: Cigarette and cigar smoke; marigolds; certain perfumes; hair spray and nail polish; old urine odours; plastic curtains; bad breath; second hand garlic; pungent underarm and foot odours; semen; untended cat-litter boxes; gasoline; bug spray; embalming fluid and eucalyptus.

DO CERTAIN COLOURS EXCITE YOU?
Yes: 44%
No: 56%

IF YES, WHAT COLOURS?
Red; black; violet; silver; orange; grey.

DO YOU WEAR FANGS?
Yes: 48%
No: 11%
Sometimes: 41%

IF YES, WHAT KIND?
Plastic; acrylic; porcelain; wax; glow-in-the-dark; synthetic material; fitted caps; teeth filed to points.

DOES SUNLIGHT BOTHER YOU?
Yes: 84%
No: 11%
Sometimes: 5%

WHAT KIND OF CLOTHING DO YOU WEAR?
Leather; velvet; jeans and a T-shirt; all black; black-and-white;

blood-red; purple and violet; grey; only silks and satins touch my skin; anything that's comfortable as long as it is black; full Edwardian gear; Goth-type clothing; depends on the occasion; I like to wear silver or gold at night; I am known for my tight corsets.

DO YOU EVER WISH YOU LIVED IN OTHER TIMES?

Yes: 13%
No: 87%

IF YES, WHEN AND WHERE?

The Wild West; Medieval times; Golden age of Atlantis; French society years 1638–1785; during the rule of Charles II; the Jazz age; late 1800s in London; Paris in the '20s or Berlin in the '30s; I would like to have been a flower child.

DO YOU THINK YOU WILL LIVE LONGER
THAN NON-VAMPIRES?

Yes: 11%
No: 89%

WERE YOU MISTREATED AS A CHILD?

Yes: 39%
No: 25%
Sometimes: 36%

CAN YOU SEE IN THE DARK?

Yes: 2%
No: 78%
Sometimes: 20%

ABRIDGED LIST OF HOBBIES: Everything Goth and Gothic; movies; TV; riding motorcycles; Wicca and witchcraft; visiting haunted houses; amusement parks and game rooms; driving; collecting weaponry; chat rooms; collecting vampire jewellery; especially bats; computer games; playing drums and guitar; visiting cemeteries; getting pierced and tattooed.

ABRIDGED LIST OF OCCUPATIONS: security guard; clerk; post-office employee; chef; housewife; student; musician; typist; LPN (Licensed Practical Nurse); theatre usher; teacher; cashier; doorman; waiter; coffee shop owner; occupational therapist; electrician; insurance salesman.